12

This volume contains the text of the three Cook Lectures, delivered by Sir Geoffrey Elton at the University of Michigan in April 1990, which reviewed various current doubts and queries concerning the writing of reasonably unbiased history. The lectures offer critical advice on how such unbiased history might be achieved, together with a general critical survey of 'fashionable' theories on the writing of history.

The Cook Lectures appear in print for the first time. Also included in the volume are reprinted versions of Sir Geoffrey's two Cambridge inaugural lectures, as Professor of Constitutional History, and as Regius Professor of Modern History. These tried to dispel, respectively, what Sir Geoffrey sees as the anti-historical fantasies current in the 1960s (but by no means yet gone), and the artificial attempt to denigrate the history of one's native country.

THE COOK LECTURES DELIVERED AT THE
UNIVERSITY OF MICHIGAN, 1990

Return to Essentials

Return to Essentials

SOME REFLECTIONS
ON THE PRESENT STATE
OF HISTORICAL STUDY

G. R. Elton

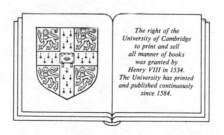

The right of the
University of Cambridge
to print and sell
all manner of books
was granted by
Henry VIII in 1534.
The University has printed
and published continuously
since 1584.

CAMBRIDGE UNIVERSITY PRESS
CAMBRIDGE   NEW YORK   PORT CHESTER
MELBOURNE   SYDNEY

Published by the Press Syndicate of the University of Cambridge
The Pitt Building, Trumpington Street, Cambridge CB2 1RP
40 West 20th Street, New York, NY 10011–4211, USA
10 Stamford Road, Oakleigh, Melbourne 3166, Australia

First published 1991

Printed in Great Britain at the University Press, Cambridge

British Library cataloguing in publication data

Elton, G. R. (Geoffrey Rudolph) *1921–*
Return to essentials: some reflections on the present state of
historical study.
I. Historiography
I. Title
907.2

Library of Congress cataloguing in publication data

Elton, G. R. (Geoffrey Rudolph)
Return to essentials: some reflections on the present state of historical
study / G. R. Elton.
p.   cm.
Cook lectures delivered at the Law School of the University of Michigan at
Ann Arbor, April 1990 – Pref.
ISBN 0 521 41098 3 (hardback)
1. History – Research. 2. Historiography. I. Title. II. Title:
Cook lectures.
D16.E44   1991
907.2 – dc20   91–8186   CIP

ISBN 0 521 41098 3 hardback

Contents

Preface

The main part of this volume, and the only part not to have appeared in print before, comprises the Cook Lectures which I delivered at the Law School of the University of Michigan at Ann Arbor in April 1990. I wish to express my profound appreciation and gratitude both for the honour of the invitation and the most friendly entertainment I received. Special thanks go to the dean, Professor Lee Bollinger, who invited me, and to old friends (more particularly Tom Green) who looked after me. I owe very special thanks to Lillian Fritzler, the dean's secretary, who went to so much trouble over me, and to Susan Kybett who made the whole thing possible by ferrying the lecturer's decaying carcase from place to place. I include here also the two inaugural lectures I delivered in the University of Cambridge on 15 February 1968 and 26 January 1984 when moving into two successive chairs of history, partly because they help to provide a little more body for the volume, but mainly to contain reflections on the reality of the labours in which I have spent nearly half a century of my professional life. But having got all this off my chest I rather hope that it is still too early to sing *Nunc dimittis*.

G.R.E.
Clare College, Cambridge
NOVEMBER 1990

The Cook Lectures
1990

1

The Claims of Theory

The main theme of these lectures will revolve around the current debates on the nature of history, debates that are especially active in the United States, but I must say at once that I cannot claim to offer an exhaustive discussion. I propose to home in on a selection of the arguments that are at present running around, and I apologize from the start to all the disputants whom I shall not be able to mention. I should also like to make it plain from the start that I shall be defending what may appear to be very old-fashioned convictions and practices. My views and attitudes were formed by some forty-five years of trying to understand the historical past and write about it, and in some people's eyes I shall unquestionably appear ossified, even dead. However, I can only preach what I believe, and I do believe in those entrenched positions concerning the reality of historical studies. Perhaps there is virtue in now and again tackling the champions of innovation and new fashion from a position of mere experience.

Where today shall we find the Queen of Sciences? In the middle ages there was never any doubt. Theology, the study of God's ways in his creation and outside it, took that place by natural right. It subsumed all sorts of studies that have since claimed autonomy: philosophy provided the means for discovering God's will; history followed God's path through past, present and future; the natural sciences expounded the details of a universe operating by the law of God; and so forth. But since the sixteenth century dethroned theology we have witnessed a struggle for the succession. The sciences

3

of nature and of man have developed in separate compartments within which there has been much rivalry for ascendancy. A hundred years ago, physics ruled the first and history came close to winning the title for the second. The experience of the past, properly and professionally studied, was recognized as the best guide to an understanding of the human condition. Other disciplines, it was agreed, could usefully contribute but only insofar as they helped to an understanding of the concrete reality of a past out of which the present had grown and from which the future might be cautiously prognosticated.

This claim on behalf of history never looked all that convincing, and before long it began to be undermined. On the one hand, the belief in a positivist history, capable of being discovered and agreed beyond all risks of partiality, retreated before various demonstrations that historians intruded the uncertainties of their own personalities into their apparently scientific work which thus came to be read as no more than a collection of individual constructs. History, some wiseacres explained, is only what this or that historian liked to put out – a superior kind of fiction. On the other hand, experience showed that historians did no better than anyone else when it came to forecasting the future: if this was so, what reliance could be placed in the idea that their work on the past equipped them with a sound understanding of human nature and the circumstances within which it operated? Once the overcharged claims of history lost credibility, attacks on it could be mounted from all sides. Some people held that there was a better sort of history to be found than that practised by historians; others went further and maintained that the less the present and future had to do with the past the better for all concerned. Both ti e e lines of thought – if thought is the right word – have cast up influential absurdities. Thus, for instance, the perfectly valid recognition that much conventional history ignored parts of the tale it claimed to tell has deteriorated into raucous claims for a history of women which leaves out men, or for a black history which deletes anything that does not fit with preconceived convictions of black separateness and indeed superiority. Past defects were to be remedied by new defective emphases, not the most promising of recipes to wave under the banner of truth. And the opinion that the present requires no past to explain it has increasingly produced attitudes hostile to historical studies on the grounds that they stand in the way of improvement. If only, so the line runs, we were free of tradition we could build a good life for everybody. Bile and innocence form a strange but powerful amalgam in this turning away from history. Not only is Clio not the queen of sciences but to many she appears as both a devil and a needless burden.

Now I think that these really extreme reactions against a knowledge of the comprehensive past, though they certainly exist, need not be treated so very seriously. This is an age of rapidly changing fashions; yesterday's buzz words are today's incomprehensible obscurities; who now remembers Marcuse and McLuhan? And though an absurd fashion is sometimes succeeded by a fashion even more absurd, generally speaking the ship does manage to right itself. Why, newly trendy historians are even heard to praise such things as diplomatic history or historical narrative which rendered their trendy predecessors apoplectic. Endeavours to escape from history altogether regularly turn out to be neither possible nor very sensible. The past is always with us and we are for ever part of it – and not only yesterday's past but also that of the retreating millennia; we cannot escape it, though we need not suppose that it shapes us in some inescapable fashion. If we try to ignore history or drive it from our minds we lose our communal memory; and why should an amnesiac society be any more satisfactory than a single person who cannot recall who or what or where he is? Trying to live in ignorance of the past does immense harm: every day's headlines tell us so as we watch people devoid of any understanding of the scenes and organizations they confront, conduct policies that are both childlike and childish. Like it or not, we live in and with history, for which reason we must give thought to the kind of history it is to be. The real threat to history as a humane, useful and respectable exercise does not come from the lunatic fringe; it operates right at the centre of the historical enterprise itself. It arises from a mixture of dissatisfactions with the limitations of any study of the past and of mistaken ideas about that study's proper function.

There are many and various attacks on what is called old-fashioned history, but I shall confine myself to three major issues, before in my third lecture turning to a positive restatement of inherited wisdom. Two of those issues reflect the overambitious dreams that afflict historians who do not see why they should not be gurus, like everybody else; the third springs from the mistaken demands of non-historians trying to read history. The first two include the call upon historians to formulate predictive laws based upon their understanding of the past, as well as the conviction that since history has to be written the only kind worth having operates within the framework of a general theory of language. The third I will call the fear of the demolished myth. Between them, and sometimes with the best will in the world, they undermine such claims to rational, independent and impartial investigation as historians can put forward for their work.

A good many people can see no virtue in history (except perhaps mere enjoyment) unless knowledge of it offers directly usable guidance to the present in its confrontation with the future. As the phrase goes, they wish to learn from history, a desire in which they have too often been encouraged by historians themselves. And they wish this learning to be precise and reliable – like the lessons of science. For them it is not enough to gain some understanding of how people may act and react in given circumstances; they call for behavioural laws to be extracted from an inspection of the past. They like such laws as that the repression of a sector of society that is rising in wealth will lead to subversion and revolution; or that the accumulation of armaments will lead to war; or that only perfect democracy will ensure peaceful relations within society; or that ideological differences will always give way before economic interests (or the other way round). We can certainly find historical examples to illustrate all such generalizations, as well as others to cast doubt. The lawmakers insist that phrases of this sort, the product of particular investigations, must have a normative function – must precisely predict what will happen – and this is where they go wrong. I remember once encountering the statement that when people have exhausted the lands they live on they will move to new lands: in effect that there is a law compelling them to do so. But there is no such law, and they do not always obey its nonexistent force. Generalizations based upon a study of past events may be convincing or contrived; what they can never be is a law of human behaviour. The trouble is that historians cannot make predictions by virtue of their science, though like anybody else they can try to prophesy as human beings, with a barely better chance of success than other people. They cannot claim powers of prediction because the secret of their success as historians lies in hindsight and argument backwards. Historians do not even know what it is they wish to analyse and understand until after it has happened; of necessity, they always reason from the situation they study to its prehistory – from what is to how it came about, not from what is to what may come of it. Thus the hunt for predictive laws contradicts the very essence of our enterprise; we leave such things to the social scientists whose scientifically based ordinances find themselves regularly ignored by disobedient mankind.

Does this mean that the simple hope enshrined in the phrase 'learning from history' is totally misplaced? It does not, but the relationship between the teaching and the learning differs a great deal from the simplicity so often imagined. A knowledge of history offers two uses to the present. It equips the living with a much wider and deeper acquaintance with the possibilities open to human thought and action than people can ever gather from their own limited experience, and it demonstrates the magnificent unpredictability of what human beings may think and do. History teaches a great deal about the existence of free will. Of course, it demonstrates the effects of circumstances, conditioning, inter-relationships, but it also demonstrates that even when this scene-setting looks remarkably alike the outcome can and will vary enormously because it arises not from environment alone but from environment used by human beings. If you incline to believe those who would reduce humanity to the mere product of discoverable nature and nurture, the study of history (provided it is free of preconceptions) will soon disabuse you. There are no human beings who do not feel the influence of the setting within which they move, but all of them also transcend their setting and in their turn affect it: what they do both within and to it remains explicable but unpredictable. The call for predictive laws thus deprives mankind of its humanity – of its power for good and evil, its ability to think and choose, its chance to triumph and to suffer. Whatever we may at times feel like, we are not the helpless playthings of a fate reducible to laws, and the variety of experiences inside the given settings – a variety revealed by an open study of the past – shows that this is so. Individuals do make history, a truth denied only by those who would rather not be saddled with the responsibility. For free will does imply a high degree of responsibility: if history teaches that we are not just the products of inescapable circumstance, it also denies us the comfort of blaming laws of behaviour for our misdeeds and false decisions.

However, if we are to absorb that very useful lesson – the lesson that frees mind and spirit from the bondages that the makers of laws are forever trying to impose upon us – we need to escape from the most insidious temptation hiding within the very concept of learning from history. That temptation lies in seeing history as essentially relevant to the present; the technique which operates that temptation is known as present-centred (sometimes presentist) history. This is what Herbert Butterfield notoriously dubbed the 'whig interpretation': it selects from the past those details that seem to take the story along to today's concerns and so reconstructs the past by means of a sieve that discards what the present and time-limited interest determine is irrelevant. The method is totally predictive: it produces the result intended because it is designed to do so. The making of convenient laws receives assistance from such simplifications, but they assuredly ruin the real historical enterprise. Though as a fact of progress through time the present has emerged from the past, it was not the task of the past to create the present, any more than it is our function today to set up a predictable future. If knowledge of the past is to entitle the historian to speak to his own day, it must not be so organized as to satisfy that day's whim; if it is to teach usefully about mankind and the human condition, it must be understood for itself and in all its variety, undetermined by the predilections of the present and unruled by it at a time when the present did not yet exist.

True, this call for an understanding of the past on its own terms has some formidable implications for the working historian confronted by an endless agglomeration of events, of circumstances, of deeds and pronouncements and reflections. How is he to create some order out of such seeming chaos, especially if he is to be barred from just constructing a simple line terminating with today's outcome? The recognition of this difficulty has produced the first great threat to unprejudiced historical study that I shall here consider: the call for a general theory organizing the past. No sense, we are told, can be made of the usual morass of historical evidence unless it is fitted into a theoretical framework: it is this framework, which exists independently of the historical detail, that will create meaning for what without it remains meaningless. Furthermore, so the argument runs, whether the historian thinks he is using such a framework or not he will inevitably be doing so as he selects his facts, makes his connections, sees significance; and it is better to be conscious of the theory employed rather than allow unrecognized predilections to direct the operation. There is weight in this argument: unconscious presuppositions have indeed done much to distort the hunt for truth about the past. What needs to be understood is the fact that recognizing one's preconceptions should enable one to eliminate them, not to surrender to them. However, the historian faces the formidable example of the social scientist who swears by theory. The social sciences tend to arrive at their results by setting up a theoretical model which they then profess to validate or disprove by an 'experimental' application of factual detail. The belief that it is only by such theories that the historian can make sense of history is not new, but it became dominant with the appearance of the French school based on the journal *Annales*. That school deliberately resorted to various theoretical models developed by such social sciences as economics, sociology and social anthropology. The result, we are assured, was to revolutionize the history of France, especially by replacing interest in the evanescent event by the extraction of the long-term structure — a neat concept because it left so much uncontrolled speculation in the hands of the historian. That influence spread after the last World War when progressive thinkers more and more took their inspiration from France, and in the United States today very few historians even question the rightness of the method. More especially they revere the name of Clifford Geertz.

And yet it is wrong, and yet it threatens the virtue of history. I am speaking, you will understand, of the great or general theories, whether or not they can be represented by mathematical models – universal theories within which all historical exposition is to be accommodated. There are, in fact, two kinds of such theories with which historians have been confronted: some are strictly ideological (they impose an overarching interpretation on the past), while others are philosophical and question the whole concept of the study of the past. Today I shall try to deal with the former. Ideological theories have been around for a long time – general interpretative schemes embodying a faith of universal validity, imposed upon the reconstruction of the past rather than derived from it. And it does not matter whether the champions of the faith claim to base it on the study of the past, because in actual fact the faith always precedes that study. In my second lecture I shall turn to some current philosophical schemes, namely the endeavours to use literary theory to destroy the reality of the past as it had previously emerged from a study of that past's relics.

Let us look at interpretative and ideological theory. It does not matter which such theory we choose: they all arise from the same ambition and all do equal harm to the independent understanding of the past. At one time Arnold Toynbee's circular model of the fortunes of civilizations commanded much respect, except in Britain where the prophet characteristically found little favour in his own country. Much was claimed for this model. Allegedly it opened a way out of the traditional historiography, preoccupied with politics and personalities, given to an excessive emphasis on Europe and its offsprings across the world, and forgetful of the subterranean forces which, some believe, really direct the fate of mankind. Thirty years ago, even dynamite could not shift Toynbee-worship in some quarters; indeed, the effective disappearance of what for a while was so hot a fever in such a short time can reassure one about the hard core of human reason. For from the first it should have been obvious (as some of us said even then) that Toynbee's theories rested on inspirational faith rather than serious study. He generalized partly from revelation and partly from the history of ancient Greece, the only so-called civilization that he had studied in the conventional way, and he consistently introduced religion into his artificial constructs because he was a mystic rather than a rationalist. His own applications of his scheme, not to mention those of his disciples, produced some remarkable absurdities which he unrelentingly defended. Thus, because his cycles demanded it, he called the seventeenth century an era of peace, even though wars of all sorts occurred in just about every one of its hundred years in just about every quarter of the globe. I should have felt certain that Toynbee has by now ceased to direct any historian's labours, if it were not for the recent biography by William McNeill which tries to restore some respectability to him as a thinker; in any case, his brief ascendancy (mainly in America and West Germany) should continue to act as a warning against theory-mongers. [1]

Thus fashions come and go. We have had history written to the model of society as a depository of the universal myth (à la Lévi-Strauss) or of coded messages saying that all forms of knowledge are only forms of power (Foucault); Benedetto Croce and R. G. Collingwood told us that all historical writing involved re-enactment in the historian's mind, a specific which pleased the history of ideas, suddenly promoted from the scullery to the drawing-room; a hundred years ago, biological theorizing derived from Charles Darwin saddled history with notions concerning evolution, the social survival of the fittest, and doctrines of racial superiority and inferiority. None of these theories wished to undermine the writing of history; they thought they were giving it shape and substance. Two things were common to them all: they made possible the rapid construction of imposing-looking edifices, and they told us much more

---

[1] For a sober but devastatingly comprehensive critique of Toynbee, the historian, see Pieter Geyl, *Debates with Historians* (Groningen, 1955), 91–178, and *Encounters in History* (London, 1963), 276–305.

about the present within which their promoters worked than about the past. Though most theory-mongers like to make our flesh creep, none of them has ever quite matched the apocalyptic visions of earlier ages with their theories. Thus the sixteenth century extracted from the Bible and the annals of sacred history the model of a true church distinguished by a continuous history of persecution, a church whose final and triumphant emergence (shortly to be expected) would signal the second coming and the end of the world. The world has not yet ended, worse luck, but then the characteristic of such major frameworks has always been their remoteness from ascertainable facts about the past.

The important question must be whether these strictures apply to what at present is the dominant theory – that theory which the prophets of theory-based history really have in mind in their instruction and propaganda. None of the faiths I have just mentioned is totally dead, though you will not find many working historians employing even the teaching of Foucault, especially now that one of his early followers, Lawrence Stone, has declared that kind of history defunct.[2] Among theorists of history, none can at present rival the Marxists for influence, particularly in the United States, in a curious fashion the last bulwark of that faith, seeing that both Russian and French historians display increasing doubts about what not so long ago was never questioned. It is too early to say what the collapse of communism in Eastern Europe will do to the Marxist view of history; so far, its chief effect has been a stunned silence among usually rather talkative scholars. Marxism claims to be the one theory of history which rests upon the empirical study of historical problems, and it fulfils the first condition demanded of all general theories by embodying a forecast of future developments – a power to prophesy. Thus, wherever one looks one can find a sizable amount of history being

2 Lawrence Stone, 'The Revival of Narrative', *The Past and the Present* (London, 1981), ch. 3.

written on the model of a progressive struggle between classes moving onward by means of revolutions, a struggle conditioned by the decisive influence of the economic sub-structure to which all other human experiences form only paraphenomena. People entertain ideas and beliefs only as by-products of their place within the economy, and all actions are designed either to advance or to prevent the revolutionary movement upward of new classes. There are some very obvious weaknesses about the Marxist framework of history, not least the fact that its prophetic capacity has misfired so very regularly. The class structure paradigm populates this kind of history with some very crude and artificial categories: feudalism, capitalism, socialism – the original Marxist trinity – still dominate, here and there slightly refined by sub-categories identifying earlier, ascendant and declining states within them. None of this, of course, describes at all precisely what we actually find in history, but the practitioners of theory-based history are always allowed a measure of Procrustean adjustment of the facts of the past, so long as the stretching and clipping are done within the framework set up by the theory. As the history of the Christian churches has demonstrated over the millennia, true faith excuses all lies.

Let me make my meaning plain. I am not denying that this kind of history has made some gains. Thanks to Darwin, we have learned better to understand the possible changes produced by an exploitation of social advantages. Toynbee may have helped to modify excessive materialism in our reading of the past, and Collingwood has helped to keep past people's own view of events before us. Marxist historiography, especially during its era of creative impact, greatly expanded the area of historians' concerns and helped illumine stresses within society. The *annalistes* have helped to break down some unnecessary barriers between the various disciplines of the mind that try to understand the human existence. You may think, as I do, that such gains (most visible where actual historical evidence is thinnest) could quite well have come without surrender to overarching theories, but it is a historical fact that they made their impact as the result of such adoptions. The danger to true history lies less in an occasional resort to illuminating generalizations than in the belief that only within them can the historian find salvation. That which first makes them attractive in the end constitutes their threat: the very fact that they offer a helpful instrument for clearing up the muddle of the past quickly turns into a conviction that the past must be reconstructed to coincide with the theory. For theories clarify and enlighten by means of a murderously circular process. Allowing a great theory to guide your steps means putting together that history that will bear out the theory. You quickly cease to be in control and become its slave. The theory directs the selection of evidence and infuses predestined meaning into it. All questions are so framed as to produce support for the theory, and all answers are predetermined by it. Historians captured by theory may tell you that they test their constructs by empirical research, but they do nothing of the sort; they use empirical research to prove the truth of the framework, never to disprove it. The reason is psychological: adoption of such a theory involves an act of faith, and acts of faith cannot afford convincing contradiction. One might think that historians might employ theories selectively, using whatever seems most likely to open up the secrets of the past without developing addiction to any one of the ways proclaimed by the theorists, but experience does not support so comforting a notion. Election of any theory as the true structure of the human past invariably means surrender to it. Universal theories are hard task-masters and do not permit dissent among their followers; indeed, they cannot afford to do so because a free testing of their claims invariably reduces them to dust.

Over the years, I have met the consequences of the

theory-frozen mind in small ways and large. Thus at the International Congress of Historical Sciences of 1960, held at Stockholm, I read a brief paper drawing attention to the fact that general notions about social control in the hands of Tudor government could not be confirmed by means of the evidence alleged (mainly acts of Parliament) because the link could not be established between the statutes and the government as supposed makers of them. A Russian delegate promptly got up and said he was baffled: surely everybody knew that acts of Parliament in the sixteenth century originated with governments known to be concerned to promote capitalism. At another meeting of that Congress, at San Francisco in 1975, the Russian delegation would not allow the translation of a Russian contribution to be read out because it had not been vetted by the faithful; it was unfortunate that the translator turned out to be a historian from Russia visiting the United States. And so it has gone on for decades – theory-dominated barriers to free study and communication. Just the other day, I read in the journal called *History Workshop* (which announces itself as edited by a socialist-feminist commune) an attempt to criticize the eminent, though late, French Marxist historian Georges Lefebvre, with a reply that made it plain that the great man had been wrong but because of his standing in the movement was not to be questioned.[3]

I will illustrate the dangers more fully from an example which is particularly fair because it involves the very events which formed the supposed empirical proof first employed in Marxist claims to offer a comprehensive framework for the understanding of history. Thereafter, the theory became sacrosanct for the followers of the faith while the details could legitimately be manhandled and misinterpreted so long as the guide lines remained in place. I am talking of the alleged change (by revolution) from feudalism to capitalism

[3] See *History Workshop* 28 (1989), 83–110.

which Marxism from the first identified in what it called the bourgeois revolution in seventeenth-century England. It was upon this paradigmatic example that the whole edifice of history as the progressive struggle of classes was first erected. This, of course, has made it imperative that its essence should be preserved: if what happened in seventeenth-century England did not demonstrate the triumph of a new bourgeois class resting upon its new capitalist mode of production and introducing a novel bourgeois ideology, the supposedly faultless empirical foundation of the faith is pitilessly exposed.

The interpretation in question originally read thus: capitalist developments in sixteenth-century England promoted the growth of an urban middle class (called the bourgeoisie) who in the civil wars of the seventeenth century overcame the earlier feudal economy based on land instead of money. The middle class fought and destroyed an aristocratic regime and thus secured the victory of capitalist principles in the mode of production, with the urban preference for trade and industry now dominating over what had been an agrarian society consisting of landowners exploiting the labours of a peasantry. In the process, the agrarian sector also went capitalist. Peasants were depressed into landless labourers, and landowners used their land solely as a source of wealth where previously it had provided a definition of status. Whereas in feudalism the classes had been interdependent throughout the hierarchic layers, with social benefits accruing to all participants, in capitalism the simple cash nexus replaced a nexus of established personal relationships. All this had been pioneered by the bourgeois classes of the towns who dominated the House of Commons, and the victory of a bourgeois Parliament over the feudal king signalled the triumph of the revolution. That revolution's ideology — epiphenomenal to the economic substructure — was the extreme form of protestantism called puritanism; it too triumphed in the revolution for which it had provided the driving force. The link between puritanism and capitalism has endured in various forms: it could be presented as oppressive by the Marxists and beneficial by Max Weber, and both were talking historical nonsense. Thus this single example sufficed to prove the Marxist theory of history, which then came to be applied, pretty rigorously, to all the events of the past, from Periclean Athens to modern Vietnam – and indeed to the future of mankind too.

Thus this first pillar of the doctrine could not be allowed to shiver since like all religions Marxism could not tolerate an erosion of its articles of faith. Yet just about every detail of the exposition I have just put before you has been progressively and comprehensively disproved. Land had been treated as a simple source of wealth certainly since the thirteenth century and probably from the beginning of time; the feudal scene involved a manifest cash nexus. On the other hand, insofar as land also constituted a measure of social standing, it retained that position in England into the later nineteenth century. Early-modern England, whose social structure did not significantly alter in the course of the seventeenth century, knew no sizable urban middle class; ascendancy in wealth, political weight and social regard remained with the aristocracy and gentry, based on landownership; successful merchants and lawyers commonly sought to invest their wealth in land and join the leading sector of the community. Capitalist practices, so called, can be discovered in any age, even as the personal relationships of landowner and tenant farmer were still manifest in recent times. Indeed, after the supposed bourgeois revolution the country's aristocracy ruled more powerfully than before: the eighteenth-century aristocracy enjoyed an independence of the monarchy which its predecessors would have envied. The notion that what emerged from the bourgeois revolution was the rule of the House of Commons has become ever more absurd in the light of research. Most spectacularly, the whole structure of puritan religion, bearer of a revolutionary and ultimately democratic message, has crumbled into nothing, to a point where now we are even excessively reluctant to speak of English puritans at all. The famous radicalism of the age, eagerly advertised by radicalized historians who were hunting truly populist movements behind the bourgeois leadership, has turned out to be the product of doctrine backed by a massive overemphasis on the inflammatory writings of a few individuals with a ready pen.

Has any of this dented the theory among those who first used it to create a comprehensible order in the confusing past? Of course not: adherents of theory do not allow facts to disturb them but instead try to deride the whole notion that there are facts independent of the observer. The Marxist scheme, giving fresh substance to the whig interpretation that preceded it, came very handy to one of the most influential scholars working on that era, R. H. Tawney, himself a Christian socialist and technically not a Marxist at all. His writings laboured under two preoccupations: his desire to put an end to capitalism in his own day, and a Marxist-derived general theory of the transformation which he thought had first created the order he hoped to help abolish. Thus he suffered from present centred demands and theory-based explanations, and even his personal goodness and magnificent prose could not overcome two such handicaps. Yet Tawney's misleading teaching about the rise of the gentry as the new middle class, or about the capitalist destruction of a socially harmonious medieval England, still informs many a textbook, thirty years after its inadequacy was first exposed. Let me emphasize that I am not trying to equip early-modern England with a universal happiness called forth by capitalist production; I find pro-capitalist history as ridiculous as anti-capitalist. Both are crutches for some current selfinterest, and neither has anything to do with history as it should be properly studied and practised. Nor do I wish to deny that the original Marxist explanation was impressive, given the state of research; I would respect those who framed it if those who came to accept had shown a willingness to allow better knowledge to affect their theses. But once a man has subscribed to a general theory as the correct way to pursue historical truth he seems to be committed to perverting the past. Some fifteen years ago, Lawrence Stone, one of Tawney's most loyal disciples, produced a book on the causes of the English revolution in which all the exploded commonplaces about a revolutionary 'class', the constitutional rebellion of the Parliament, and the revolutionary creed of puritanism reappeared.[4] Since it continues to serve as a text for school students and undergraduates, the principal theory of the book remains well entrenched despite the much better understanding long since obtained.

One reason for the survival of the Marxist structure lies in the immense productivity of Christopher Hill who unlike those other scholars is an avowed believer in the faith. His many books and articles, published over some thirty years, have most ingeniously developed the orthodoxy in an increasingly sophisticated adaptation of the unchanging guide lines to an expanding knowledge of detail. His impressive campaign not unnaturally created a highly influential orthodoxy, expressly based on the Marxist theory of history as a succession of conflicts between classes. But the progress of Hill's own research imposed a most peculiar development upon this universal explanation. It being axiomatic that the revolution must be called bourgeois, it became necessary to identify the social class which could be seen to carry a bourgeois ideology and bourgeois commercial practices into effect. The urban and mercantile class soon proved inadequate to the task which thus devolved upon the artisans of the towns and the yeomen of the countryside – what Hill called 'the industrious sort'. This loose term had at least the advantage of being current, in other senses,

---

[4] Lawrence Stone, *The Causes of the English Revolution 1529–1642* (London, 1972); see my review in *Historical Journal* 16 (1973), 205–8.

during the seventeenth century which, after all, had never heard of the bourgeois in England. However, the industrious sort also proved unwilling to carry the burden of a historic mission, and even Hill recognized that the puritans, left in charge of the field, would be hard to convert into a class. He therefore turned towards the unsuccessful revolutionaries – the class of the underdog – whose radical sectarianism with its allegedly democratic beliefs aimed to revolutionize the world. Among them the so-called Ranters, reportedly possessed of the wildest notions, were given pride of place. Unhappily it has now been discovered that the Ranters never existed as a sect with a following; the mouthings of two or three fools were exploited by an enterprising publisher looking for titillating material to sell to a salacious readership. This discovery has produced a sort of supernova effect within the Marxist camp, leaving in the end only a black hole. One alleged class after another has let the historian down.[5]

Hill is a serious historian who has done a great deal of work, and he has had many students some of whom became

[5] For Hill's work see especially *The English Revolution* (London, 1940); *Economic Problems of the Church from Archbishop Whitgift to the Long Parliament* (Oxford, 1956) (but see R. O'Day and F. Heal, eds., *Princes and Paupers in the English Church 1500–1800* (London, 1981)); *Society and Puritanism in Pre-Revolutionary England* (London, 1964); *Intellectual Origins of the English Revolution* (Oxford, 1965) (but see John Morgan, *Godly Learning: Puritan Attitudes towards Reason, Learning and Education 1560–1640* (Cambridge, 1986)); *God's Englishman: Oliver Cromwell and the English Revolution* (London, 1970); *Milton and the English Revolution* (London, 1977); *The World Turned Upside Down* (London, 1972); *The Century of Revolution 1603–1714* (London, 1961). For the removal of the Ranters see J. C. Davis, *Fear, Myth and History: The Ranters and the Historians* (Cambridge, 1986); the counter-attack on this by E. P. Thompson, in *The London Review of Books*, was distinguished by ignorance and devotional bile. J. H. Hexter, *On Historians* (London, 1979), 227–51, constitutes a perceptive analysis of the faults in Hill's historical methods which have enabled him to maintain his thesis.

loyal followers. Why, then, have all those constructs col-
lapsed? Wedded to a comprehensive theory which depended
on the existence of social classes in conflict, he could not
admit that seventeenth-century England contained no
classes; its structure can be analysed in various ways – by
localities, by occupations, by wealth, by status – but never
by class. Wedded to the theory of genuine revolution, he
could not admit that even a civil war and the temporary
abolition of the monarchy did not necessarily bring about
such a revolution; but in fact, none had happened. The
theory directed the selection of the evidence all of which
came from writings, pamphlets, sermons and such-like, that
is from material of comment and not of the event. Selection
guided by theory produced the usual effect: support for an
answer worked out in advance, but an answer which the vast
masses of genuine evidence ignored by Hill have by stages
rendered untenable. However, the true believer cannot surrender his theory, and Hill's most recent statements concerning the issues continue to proclaim the victory of a
bourgeois revolution. As I understand it, he now agrees that
the ends allegedly achieved cannot be identified as the
ambitions of a bourgeois sector and that indeed nothing to
be described as a bourgeois class in the Marxist sense existed
at the time. But, we are told, this does not entail the
disappearance of a bourgeois revolution, so long as the
outcome can be said to look like what the historian has from
the first labelled with that name.

You may think that I am spending too long over one
erring colleague, but I need to establish my case. I could at
length explore the effects of theory-worship upon other
Marxist historians of England – all highly intelligent, all in
command of a sizable following, all of them cocooned in
their fictions. Those who insist that historians should
operate by means of large interpretative theories do so on the
grounds that only theories will bring out the mechanisms
that govern the past and that therefore without theory the

historian is a mere antiquary. In the case of Hill's revolution, the mechanism, once discovered by theory-free study, totally denied the theory, but the historian preserved the theory by discarding its supposed role in opening the meaning of the evidence. This sort of thing, much commoner than you may think, can happen only in countries where historical research is not controlled by the state and where therefore the theorist's history gets criticized and demolished by historians working properly. Theorists deceive themselves if they suppose that they would do that work anyway: scholars who believe that they will abandon their comprehensive theory if research invalidates it contradict experience. Max Weber advanced his ideas linking protestantism and capitalism as a working hypothesis; the moment that was criticized it turned into a profound conviction, the more firmly adhered to the more preposterous it turned out to have been. It takes a mental revolution equal to a spiritual conversion to separate a devotee from his theory, and the chances are that that will happen only if another theory stands by to catch the convert.

All these great historical theories enshrine forms of a faith, a faith either explicitly or implicitly religious. Even as Marxists adhere to the religion of the revolution of the class struggle, even though they cannot uncover the conditions or consequences called for by the doctrine, so current feminist historians subscribe to a universal theory according to which every improvement in the condition of males was achieved by causing deterioration of conditions for females, though only the crudest and most inadequate simplification of history has ever been offered to underwrite this notion.[6] The lesson is plain, but it is also devastating: all forms of religious belief threaten the historian's ability to think for himself and to investigate the reality of the past. The historian, it seems, if he values his integrity, must be a

[6] Joan Kelly, *Women, History, and Theory* (Chicago, 1984).

professional sceptic — a scholar who cannot accept anything merely on the instruction of a faith. If in fact he (as many do) believes in a real religion he is particularly at risk and needs to be specially on his guard.

I am aware that I shall be accused of vile prejudice — of denouncing Marxism because my taste in politics goes counter to communism, and of denouncing faith because I do not adhere to one. But I am also aware that this is not true. If I warn you against religion it is because any student of the sixteenth century knows what religion has done to the historiography of that age, and if I attack the Marxist theory of history it is because at present it forms the most influential, and therefore most damaging, of these doctrinal structures. I feel exactly the same way about the Christian theory according to which history exemplifies the hand of God leading mankind through tests and tribulations to the Last Day. I am equally unhappy about the so-called progress theory of history — a theory which by a highly tendentious selection of the evidence demonstrates straight lines of betterment, especially in constitutional freedoms, through the ages — ending, predictably, in whatever English or American practice receives most conventional praise. I am not concerned to maul anything; I only wish to rescue the study of history from being mauled by its molesters. True practitioners must cultivate a respect for the past in its own right and an open-minded scepticism towards all theories, large and small, those of others and their own. If such respect and scepticism are available only to those who tend to agnosticism in religion and conservative views in politics, so be it, but I have no reason to think that this is actually true. Possibly a conservative temperament, willing to accept life on earth as it is with all its imperfections, finds such attitudes easier to achieve than does the progressive temperament, ever anxious to promote changes that will make things better. But even progressive and optimistic historians can, if they try, avoid the pitfalls of the general theory which demands the service of acolytes. The will is all.

I repeat that the objections I have raised concern supposedly comprehensive theories used in approaching and
ordering the evidence: previously constructed schemes
which guide the research ostensibly designed to test them.
The alternative to this is not, as we sometimes hear, a merely
mindless accumulation of detail; the alternative lies in particular explanatory schemes extracted by unpreconditioned
research and applicable to particular cases only. Such theories are neither universal nor predictive, though they may
stimulate research into sufficiently similar cases. One fundamental difference lies in the fact that the second demands no
faith and leaves the possibility of abandonment open. Even
the mind that first framed it must remain open to calls for
revision, however pleased it was with the original exposition. I speak with a certain amount of feeling. Some forty
years ago I thought that I had discovered a period in English
history – the 1530s – when certain people and certain
circumstances co-operated to produce a major transformation in the structure and purpose of the state. Unfortunately I called it a 'Tudor Revolution', at first 'in Government', but in due course in every aspect of public and many
aspects of private life (as for instance in the development of
language). I should have known better, for I meant no more
than drastic but also fundamental change. I did not realize
that 'revolution' is a term protected by patent rights held by
those for whom real revolutions, deserving of the name,
involve popular uprisings. Anyway, I then thought that I
had found a theory to organize the history of the sixteenth
century in particular and other surrounding periods in
general. Much work has been done since, by others as well as
by myself, and the original theory looks a bit frayed. I have
had to change my mind on quite a number of points, even if
I cannot yet see that those who deny the whole concept have
proved their case. But at least I was able to control the
theory rather than be controlled by it, nor have I tried to

universalize it beyond the area where the evidence first made me formulate it. The theory proved a useful and usable tool of analysis which had been put together by the basic experimental work — work done before the theory had been thought of. That seems to me the correct relationship between research and generalization in history, and I would claim that my experience proves that it is entirely possible to work thus and get valid results.

So much for the theories offered as necessary for the work of historical reconstruction — the work of making structured sense out of the chaos of detail. In my next lecture I propose to turn to those who have come to conclude that there is no road back to a truth of the past — to those, that is, who have absorbed the apparently widespread conviction that certain extravagances current among students of literature render all forms of objective study impossible and therefore disable the historian from ever achieving what for a long time now he has stated to be his ambition. Ideological theories create preconditioned convictions about the historical past; philosophical theories deny that the historical past can ever be reconstituted. The first undermine the historian's honesty, the second his claims to existence.

2

The Burden of Philosophy

I have so far tried to show that what I have called ideological theory threatens the work of the historian by subjecting him to predetermined explanatory schemes and thus forcing him to tailor his evidence so that it fits the so-called paradigm imposed from outside. The alternative onslaught committed by theory is in its way more devastating still because it denies the very possibility of treating the past as having happened independently from the historian who supposedly is at work on it. While the first form of theory submits to the constructs of the social sciences, the second accepts service with psychology and language studies, out of which there have grown special forms of literary criticism. The first attacks history through its substantive content, the second gets under its guard through the fact that the historian has to express himself in words. Partly because this second attack is relatively recent, and partly because it took its origin from characteristically charismatic Frenchmen, it is in some ways more comprehensively menacing — or at least one less warded off so far. Victims of the virus acquire a dangerous sense of intellectual well-being, a cocooned contentment. It has proved particularly insidious in the United States where the intellectual community (as it styles itself) is always inclined to accept most humbly the latest fashions, and it has particularly infected the history of ideas which by its very nature is liable to lose contact with reality. When the subject of study is almost entirely confined to other people's arrangement of words, theories of literary criticism, however dubious in themselves, naturally assume importance.

The beacons along this dangerous road were lit by certain philosophers, especially Heidegger and Adorno, and by successive waves of literary critics from structuralists through post-structuralists to deconstructionists among whom the great names appear to be Saussure, Barthes and Derrida, with Foucault acting as the agent who transferred the theories to the historians. German philosophy and French *esprit* – a dangerous cocktail because while the former may be incomprehensible it looks wise, and the latter demonstrates that the absurd always sounds better in French. Much of what faces us now took its origin in the perfectly correct reaction against simple-minded notions of objectivity and the recognition that history is written by historians, but predictably attacks on one extreme position would not stop until another equally extreme one had been developed. However, on this I hope to say a bit more in my third and last lecture; today I am more concerned with the consequences than the roots of this array of subtleties. A conveniently succinct and lucid exposition of the obscurities involved in deconstruction appeared last year in the *American Historical Review*, from the pen of Professor David Harlan, who has also published one short study of the American clergy in the eighteenth century, based on the reading of pamphlets and sermons.[1] The conceit of those theorists which identifies power with knowledge has attracted the more fanatical feminists who are convinced that traditional historians have twisted all their accounts into support for what is called patriarchy; conveniently, the same issue of that *Review* contains a run-down of this variant of the theory by the reasonably fanatic Joan Wallach Scott who manages to marry deconstruction and Marxism, which is like spiking

---

[1] David Harlan, 'Intellectual History and the Return of Literature', *American Historical Review* 94 (1989), 581–609; in 1980 he published his doctoral dissertation presented at the University of California, Irvine, under the title *The Clergy and the Great Awakening in New England*.

vodka with LSD.[2] Between them, Harlan and Scott give us a sufficient picture of what is involved.

However, before we turn to this latest manifestation of the destructive effect that psychology married to literary criticism can have upon the labours of historians, it seems advisable to take a look at what until fairly recently looked like the up-to-date versions of this form of attack. One comes from philosophy, the other from literary studies, and both have attracted much favourable respect. The philosopher is Hans Georg Gadamer who held that truth 'is not a relation between an individual perceiver and the world' but 'an agreement reached through critical discussion'.[3] To this we can only say that to us truth is what irrevocably lies in the past and sets the standard of knowledge to which we aspire without thinking that we shall ever reach it to everybody's satisfaction. The existence of uncertainty and disagreement does not abolish the truth of the past event. Gadamer, in fact, introduced that source of confusion which seems to cause much trouble especially to historians of ideas (a vociferous minority).[4] He it was who held when a historian uses the word truth he means to endow the writings of the past with an abstract and provable possession of that quality. It follows that historical study should aim to remove itself from the past into the present, but it also follows that unlike the owner of a critical theory the historian has no means of establishing such a claim. Therefore some historians embrace critical theory – a chimerical lifeline. But when the historian speaks of truth in connection with the writings of Plato or Hobbes or Marx he means to discover what exactly and when, and perhaps for what reason, Plato and Hobbes

[2] *American Historical Review* 94 (1989), 680–92.
[3] On Gadamer see, for example, William Outhwaite in *The Return of Grand Theory in the Human Sciences*, ed. Q. Skinner (Cambridge, 1985), 21–39.
[4] Compare J. Ibbett, 'Gadamer, Application and the History of Ideas', *History of Political Thought* 8 (1987), 545–55.

and Marx put down the words that survive as their writings. He may also wish to discover whether what they reported accurately reflected what had happened. But he is not concerned to discover in their writings some eternal truth: this is not nor can it be of the slightest interest to him as a historian, whatever his feelings may be as a true believer in this or that religion. It is for this reason that the whole business of transferring the principles of scriptural exegesis – the arcane science called hermeneutics – is totally irrelevant to the practice of history, though it has lately crept into discussions concerning the analysis and understanding of historical documents, or 'texts', as the non-historians prefer to call them. Hermeneutics, according to the best dictionaries, is the science of interpretation more specifically of the Bible. That is to say, it is a body of principles developed in the endeavour to find a coherent and cohesive meaning within a very diverse and varied body of writings, on the assumption that those writings derive from a single author, namely God, and must therefore carry a single message. On the other hand, a historical study of all those components of Holy Writ recognizes that they were produced and preserved by human agencies over a long period of time and need interpreting within the context of their origins and purposes, with the result that we drift further away from the truth the more we force them into a single and all-embracing framework. Hermeneutics is the science which invents meaning; historical study depends on discovering meaning without inventing it. Hermeneutics seeks to reduce variety to cohesiveness, while history accepts the probability of unpredictable variety. Therefore, hermeneutics is a term not only not applicable to the historian's operation but positively hostile to it; its use enables the student to impose meaning on his materials instead of extracting meaning and import from them. I shall come back to this. The truth we seek is the truth of the event and all that surrounds it, not the possibility that a truth abstracted from the event is being proclaimed and can be teased out by the techniques of the critic. Once this essential distinction is grasped we can leave the philosophers and critics to play their games and attend to out proper task.

Next we might as well pay heed to the daddy of the endeavour to treat historical exposition as a form of literary discourse and no more. Hayden White (who relied on several literary theorists but above all, it seems, on Northrop Frye) called his ruminations metahistory, a thing near to but not identical with history; but this frank and modest avowal has not prevented his work from affecting real history itself, to a point where White too no longer draws the line. It would in fact seem that the word is read to signify a form of study which goes beyond mere history and is therefore superior to it, even as metaphysics is read to mean thought superior to a mere physical description of reality. (Actually, as you probably know, metaphysics is so called because in the received canon of Aristotle's writings his treatise on philosophy came after – *meta* – his treatise on physics; no value judgement was intended). White's metahistory turns out to be somewhat specialized in the range of history considered, but behind the discussion assuredly lies a universal theory about the writing of history. In the book he confined himself to an analysis of four historical philosophers and four practising historians, all of the nineteenth century: it is a specialized piece of intellectual history. The categories he uses for analysis also come in fours, but none of it, alas, stands squarely on all fours.

Metahistory consummated White's intellectual pilgrimage but did not initiate it. Having produced various modest works in the history of ideas, he published in 1966 an interesting manifesto which he called 'The Burden of History'.[5] It became evident that he had undergone the sort of experience that we associate with the road to Damascus: a

[5] *History and Theory* 5 (1966), 111–34.

shock had opened his eyes to the insufficiencies of the life he had been leading. As he saw it, historians had ceased to command the respect which not so long before had been theirs because they had failed to identify their position precisely and to acquire an image justified in theory. White rather surprisingly went back to the long-dead dispute whether history was a science or an art, a dispute that even in America had ceased to attract most practitioners who found it perfectly easy to accept that, insofar as those terms meant anything, they could be involved in one or the other as circumstances and need demanded. But to White, now seeing with the pitiless eyes of the new convert, historians had thereby ceased to command intellectual respect; their feeble efforts to avoid commitment to one or the other of that supposedly antagonistic pair had been rumbled. They were, he alleged, provoking general resentment, though on closer inspection that general feeling appeared to be entertained solely by literary scholars who thought that historians' emphasis on ascertainable fact had relegated any involvement in fiction to a lower circle of Hell. Thus, White proclaimed, historians needed to 're-establish the dignity of historical studies on a basis that will make them consonant with the aims and purposes of the intellectual community at large'. Now that his eyes were open he saw only arrogance around him, and he attacked what he had come to see as the leading practitioners – men who thought themselves sane and demonstrated their sanity by 'finding the simple in the complex and the familiar in the strange'. To him, it would appear, the whole landscape now looked immensely complicated and distinctly alien, and while I think he should have realized that the spectacles he had put on were responsible for this I would nevertheless respect his right to feel so perturbed. He had come to think that what at the time he called the present generation needed above all 'a willingness to confront heroically the dynamic and disruptive forces in contemporary life'. 'Discontinuity,' he exclaimed, 'dis-

ruption, and chaos is [*sic*] our life.' That voice is manifestly
the voice of the 1960s in an American surprised to find that
the anodyne consensus of the previous twenty years had
come under attack from a new generation rebelling all over
the place. His reference to an intellectual community dis-
concertingly reflects what particularly troubled observers
from outside the States at the time – the disarray of academic
departments in the face of the student revolution and all
that. The disarray did affect the history departments more
than most as they took a great deal of blame for misleading
the noisy champions of supposed freedoms: the 'intellectual
community' wished the historians out of the way and many
remained in a state of shock for quite a while. It was a time
when the inadequacies of people who had had it a bit too
easy were being shown up, and when the last thing to be
found in those quarters was anything resembling heroics.
Truth to tell, White's penny-whistle did not call for
heroism; it demanded submission to the fashion of the
moment, and as that moment passed (as so very quickly it
did, something that proper historians ought to have
expected to happen) the folly of such a total surrender
became ever more plain. Panic is not a good guide to action,
even in an intellectual community.

Seven years later, in 1973 when the age of rebellion had
joined the historical past, Hayden White published the
book that I have already alluded to and that was to make him
a centre of attraction among those who believed that the
work of the historians depended on the historian rather than
the work, so that its study should be reduced to a study of
the manner in which historians accounted for the past.[6] We
hear there no more about the burden of history, or of a heroic
confrontation of chaos; instead we learn that the writing of
history happens in one of four modes, identified as metaphor, synecdoche, metonymy and irony – all of them

[6] *Metahistory: The Historical Imagination in Nineteenth-Century Europe*
(Baltimore, 1973).

figures of speech characterized by allusiveness rather than precision and immediacy. So far as I am able to judge, White had come to the conclusion that historians used these indirect methods in accounting for the past so as to avoid commitment in the battle between science and art, but I may well be mistaken; I remain somewhat baffled by this welter of terms invented by the rhetoricians of ancient Greece. On the other hand, it is quite clear that White holds history proper and the philosophy of history to be the same thing, with the philosophers making explicit what in the historians' work is merely implicit. In view of the sad fact that virtually no philosopher of history seems ever to have tried to work out a historical problem in the manner of the genuine historian – they display instead a remarkable skill in picking on the uninstructive verbiage of the textbooks for their illustrations of historical work – I cannot find this identification altogether convincing. However, it then comes as no surprise to learn that the work of Ranke and Burckhardt owes its repute not to 'the nature of the "data" they used to support their generalizations or the theories they invoked in explaining them'; what matters, it appears, are 'the consistency, coherence, and illuminative power of their respective visions of the historical field'. Furthermore, since nothing depends on the materials employed or the reasoning applied, these historians also cannot be refuted; and if there is no valid argument possible, it must follow that all reconstructions are of equal value, which means of no value independent of writer and reader. Quite frankly, this is altogether meaningless verbiage, testifying only to a general lack of experience in trying actually to write serious history, and more especially history beyond the narrow confines of the history of ideas. There is no reason why great historians (or indeed lesser ones) should not have their manner of thinking and operating investigated, but such studies are pointless unless the investigator can demonstrate that he knows at first hand what working on the materials

left to us by the past really means. To this point I hope to
return in my last lecture.

However, to a generation anxious to bridge the gap
between history and literature (if only in order to regain
respect for historians among literary critics) White's mysterious message proved attractive. At least it did in America
where the fact that he cited Sartre, Lévi-Strauss and Foucault
among his mentors naturally helped. Six ponderous essays
were devoted to analysing the mystery he had created, in a
Beiheft to *History and Theory* published in 1980.[7] As it turned
out, even scholars anxious to discern virtue in the book could
not do very much with it. Hans Kellner rightly noted that
White offers only a predetermined and prejudged discourse;
his manner of proceeding operates inside a system carefully
closed at all points by the operator. Typically enough, the
cry for freedom produced a general denial of free rights for
the greater glory of a universal system, a religion; at least
White proved that his experience on the road to Damascus
had turned him into a prophet, even if only a minor one.
The one person among his critics in that *Beiheft* who similarly inclines to a linguistic analysis of historical writing did
him more harm than the rest who never quite understood
how his mind worked. Nancy S. Struever approved of
White's resort to what that corner of the field calls rhetoric
but maintained that his foursome had mistaken the technical
rhetorical device used by historians: they, she said, relied in
fact on argument and not on metaphor and all the rest. This
blinding glimpse of the obvious is correct enough: historians
always, in their reconstructions, argue with the evidence,
with themselves and with other historians. Unfortunately,
however, this esoteric correction still does not do what
White once set out to do: it does not advance the renown of
the study of history or justify historians' claims to be heard
by and within the intellectual community. In truth, alas, all

[7] *History and Theory*, *Beiheft* 19 (1980).

this philosophizing discourse wheels pointlessly inside an empty skull and an arching empyrean. Now there you have quite a fair example of both synecdoche and metaphor, for what they are worth.

So much for Hayden White. Let me now turn to the disciples, or victims, of the latest fashion in literary criticism − or rather more commonly the last but one such fashion. Disciples do have a terrible time to keep up with what the moving finger writes. The general import of the teaching purveyed from the deconstructionist quarter sounds extremely subtle but is in fact simplicity itself. It is that nothing written can be read as meaning what it seems to say: it always needs decoding in some way or other. (What happens when a deconstructionist, serving in a bakery, is asked for a loaf of bread?) Anyway, that 'some way or other' is conditioned by the fact that only the mind of the decoder matters. Now deconstructionists are persuaded that they have come to demolish the smug assumptions of the bourgeois world and have found a weapon with which to win a battle that Marxism had looked like losing − and incidentally seems now to have lost in once communist countries. They hide their ultimate purpose behind theories of language which remove all agreed meanings because agreement signifies surrender to what is then called establishment ascendancy.[8] It is actually quite possible to suppose that it all started as a great big joke taking off the solemnities of intellectuals, but if that once was the case I fear solemnity won the day. Thus, in the understanding of any text, which means any collection of words, it is the decoder who decides what the supposed author has said, which means that the decoder alone − and not the author − is worth reading. This simple triumph of monumental egotism comes to us dressed up in the jargon of German philosophy and the imagery of

[8] I am grateful to Professor Norman F. Cantor for letting me see the summary of his discussion of these mental aberrations, entitled 'At last! Deconstruction made easy'.

French discourse – a discourse nowadays in which metaphors regularly do duty for rational thinking. Thus, to take an example, Le Roy Ladurie, a much admired historian but quite a prophet for dubious causes, can suppose himself to have contributed a historical explanation when he likens the expansion of the world's population to an exploding galaxy, or the social structure of a village to a magnetic field. But behind the esoteric language and the outward garment of philosophizing lies no more than the famous *pronunciamento* of Humpty Dumpty in Lewis Carroll's *Alice in Wonderland*: 'When I use a word ... it means just what I choose it to mean – neither more nor less.' Nor, therefore, does the word have to have the same meaning twice running: it signifies only what at any given moment the critic says it does. You might suppose that all this decoding obeyed some general rules, if only in order to make it more likely that two different deconstructionists come up with the same answer, but so far as I can see any such device would support the ascendancy of what is under attack – that is to say, the rule of reason. I should like you to remember this because it is a point to which we shall have to return.

Professor Harlan has in effect swallowed this product of literary criticism whole; he needs it because he wishes to rid himself of the contextual prescriptions in the analysis of texts which are associated with, and propagated by, Quentin Skinner, who was seeking to provide firm guidelines for the understanding of past political thinkers. But, of course, such guidelines can be deconstructed as mere assertions of power, even when they are as sensible as Skinner's are – or perhaps especially when they are as sensible as that. Skinner has told us repeatedly that if we want to know what Machiavelli or Hobbes meant – what they were trying to say – we have to gain as perfect a grasp as possible of their own language and of the setting – historical, ideological, possibly economic and biological, and certainly political – within which they worked. Because they were thinking from within their own world, we have to follow them into that world. But this is surely just the general recipe for coming to grips with the past, and when Skinner put his doctrines to work, especially in his *Foundations of Modern Political Thought* (1978), he seemed to me to produce excellent and pellucid examples of what ever since the work of John Neville Figgis in the 1890s has been the best procedure for historians of political thought, and by implication of such other forms of intellectual history as that of literature or science. He placed the thinkers of the fifteenth to seventeenth centuries as operating within the mental conventions and conditions of the fifteenth to seventeenth centuries, thereby making them both comprehensible to the modern reader and convincing in their own terms. Thus adherence to what a trifle grand-iloquently is now called the principle of contextualism produced good history – clear and understandable in the hands of Quentin Skinner, a bit obfuscated in those of his ally John Pocock, whose preferred obscurity of language makes him at times sound like the modern critics of the contextual method but in fact more accurately reproduced the complex-ities embraced by the writers whom he was displaying from within their context in history.

Now this, I fear, is exactly what Harlan, obedient to his guides Derrida and Barthes augmented by the ponderous Hans Georg Gadamer, says is wrong. Because, on the one hand, the meaning of any bit of language is to be determined by the reader from within his own world of thought and understanding (on the grounds that the reader cannot think in any other way), and because, on the other (to quote Gadamer) no historian can ever rid himself of 'inherited prejudices and preconceptions', it is a mere illusion that by restoring the writer to his context we can recover what he was saying. Harlan (as his critic, David A. Hollinger, also points out in the same issue of the *American Historical Review*)[9] rather

---

[9] 'The Return of the Prodigal: The Persistence of Historical Knowledge', *American Historical Review* 94 (1989), 610–21.

ostentatiously avoids mentioning any historical writing. Instead of being shown by example that the Skinner recipe cannot and does not work, we are moved into the realm of imaginary literature, in a very odd attempt to equate the historian with Herman Melville's Ahab, and his search for the truth of the past with the hunting of the white whale. This does not appear to be a counsel of despair but something to be proud of, and yet it quite ostentatiously avoids the supposed realities of the argument. However, leaving aside a construct – calling indeed for deconstruction – which indicts current methods of writing the history of ideas without specifying a single piece of historical writing, let us note the conclusion at which Harlan arrives: 'We should not expect,' he murmurs, 'to encounter now-dead authors in the body of their texts.' No reason is offered for this distressing abdication which simply follows from the dictates and edicts of certain literary critics whose chief characteristic would appear to be that they do not want the author to be read at all except through the distorting, and ever changing, lenses of their own private lorgnettes. What this does, of course, is to elevate personal quirks into commanding guides: it is a form of enslavement and moreover one for which no rational explanation is given.

Treating past ideas and writers about ideas out of their context – with no regard to an understanding of the setting – not surprisingly is likely to lead to fairly disastrous consequences. Allow me to cite two examples which came my way as a reviewer. The less damaged undertaking was Judith H. Anderson's study of biographical writings of the sixteenth and seventeenth centuries in which she included the Venerable Bede and William Shakespeare.[10] This is an intelligent, quite sensible, and in the main often interesting contribution by a scholar who appears to have trained as a

[10] Judith H. Anderson, *Biographical Truth: The Representation of Historical Persons in Tudor-Stuart Writing* (New Haven and London, 1984).

literary critic and acknowledges the guidance of Hayden White and Stephen Greenblatt, two scholars that non-historians are bound to regard as historians with whom they can discuss things. But Dr Anderson's method relied entirely on textual analysis with no effort made to understand authors and writings as part of the historical scene; in analysing the meaning of the texts or what the authors were trying to do, she ignored all forms of context to the point where those writers could have lived at any time in history – or never. This, of course, meant leaving out any understanding of the social life of the time and therefore the discovery of imagined truths which an hour of reading actual history would have shown up for what they are. Thus when Dr Anderson found George Cavendish, in his *Life of Wolsey*, recording conversations that took place within window embrasures she divined at once a 'growing innerness' in her author. If she had understood the circumstances of Tudor palaces with their large and gloomy rooms, circumstances which induced people talking to each other to seek the light and privacy of those window spaces, she would not have invented such an absurdity. Her method even barred her from studying the history of her texts: she treated Thomas More's *History of Richard III* as a finished work, capable of being assessed as one such, despite the surviving drafts which show that More meant to continue the story beyond Richard's coronation to his death. It is really sad to see potentially good work spoiled by such wide-eyed innocence of any historical method. But much worse consequences befell Robert K. Faulkner's book on Richard Hooker on whom he had lavished much thought and labour.[11] Faulkner allowed his mentors to persuade him that temporal context – a place in time – meant nothing. Thus not only could and should Hooker – an author whose life's work was directed by his debates with contemporaries – be studied without refer-

[11] Robert K. Faulkner, *Richard Hooker and the Politics of a Christian England* (Berkeley, 1981).

ence to his time and place and setting, but all other writers that Dr Faulkner found himself referring to, from Aristotle through David Hume to Sir John Neale, had to be assembled in the same timeless frame, all conversing, in the most improbable manner conceivable, with one another. In this case, alas, the disastrous method produced only uselessness in the product, the gloom being lightened here and there when Dr Faulkner inadvertently reported items of common knowledge as though they represented new discoveries.

I cite you these examples not because I want to be nasty to some young scholars, sadly misled by the theory-mongers, but because they do confirm that in battling against people who would subject historical studies to the dictates of literary critics we historians are, in a way, fighting for our lives. Certainly, we are fighting for the lives of innocent young people beset by devilish tempters who claim to offer higher forms of thought and deeper truths and insights – the intellectual equivalent of crack, in fact. Any acceptance of those theories – even the most gentle or modest bow in their direction – can prove fatal, as Harlan quite sufficiently demonstrates. Nor can I feel that Professor Hollinger's answer provides a sufficient shield against the cancerous radiation that comes from the forehead of Derrida and Foucault (stop that metaphor). He rightly notes that 'trends in literary theory come and go with some rapidity', a fact which tends to have the result that obedient historians are too often one or two turns behind the latest theory. It is therefore worth notice that among literary critics what they call historicism is just at present gaining ground! And Hollinger is also right in charging Harlan with an 'inability to distinguish his own agency from that of the texts he cites': that is to say, Harlan obeys the Humpty-Dumpty principle. But unfortunately Hollinger does not go far enough; he still confines the discussion to intellectual history, as though that branch of the work in some way enjoyed an independent existence, and he says nothing on the right method of studying texts – unless we suppose that he is content to follow the somewhat high-falutin lines mapped out in their theories by Skinner and Pocock, which nonetheless have the virtue of respecting the past and producing good history. In consequence, Harlan is able to extricate himself from the hole into which he had stumbled: in replying, he suddenly admits the need to consider old thinkers within their contexts but claims a special ambition for himself and a few people like him. They are not really offering us a last word on the right way to see the past; that is unattainable except through the distorting lenses of the modern observer who in the end alone matters. What they are after is something quite different and could never have been guessed at from Harlan's first article. They wish to devise a form of narrative which would bring history and non-historical studies under one roof.[12] I confess that this leaves me baffled. Why should one accommodate other forms of story-telling within the canon of historical reconstruction? Does Harlan, deprived of his historian's freedom by the deconstructionists, wish to extend to the historian the liberties open to the writer of fiction? True, there are some historians who drift over to the fictitious, but they do so without (I hope) realizing it. In any case, Harlan is very much mistaken if he thinks that only the literary critics of his devotion offer a bridge between history and literature – but that is another topic that must wait.

What emerges, painfully, from these debates is a very serious problem. Those who preach the virtues of these recent styles of literary criticism, naturally believe themselves to have learned new truths about the manner in which the human mind absorbs and reacts to reality. However, when listening to some quite extraordinarily unreal guides they are in effect only seeking the satisfaction and propagation of their own selves. They come to think that only their own existence is real; everything else exists only in

---

[12] *American Historical Review* 94 (1989), 624.

relation to that one central fact. This is an attitude entirely proper to the adolescent mind, trying to come to terms with the world, but it is not a stance that should survive growing up. One of the possible uses of history is to assist in that growing-up process, by reminding the individual that he or she is very far from being the centre of the universe. But to these disciples of total relativism history matters only insofar as it contributes to their own lives, thoughts and experiences – those identities which they regard as singularly important and wish us to take very seriously. To me, I fear, this is the ultimate heresy. For the historian is in the first place concerned with the people of the past – with *their* experiences, thoughts and actions – and not with the people of the present, least of all with himself. This does not mean that I consider it possible for him to exclude himself from the enterprise called studying the past: of course, the history he tells has to be processed through his mind and pen. But, as I hope to show in my last lecture, that involvement is not equal to dominance; it does not mean that he stands at the centre of the historical reconstruction (Croce and Collingwood were utterly wrong); it does not mean, to cite Gadamer once more, that he cannot escape from his prejudices and preconceptions. That risk he runs only when he obeys the false guides with their destructive message that we have here been considering.

In the study of history, a primary preoccupation with the present is thus always dangerous, a danger which appears in yet another form of the crisis which allegedly afflicts the enterprise. History has through the millennia served present-day causes of a different kind, causes which did not attempt to provide universal guidelines for action by means of predictive laws or specialize in fitting the self-centred historian within the even more self-centred milieu of the intellectual community. People have usually sought in history a justification for their convictions and prejudices; whole nations have over the centuries lived in cocoons of convenient myths the demolition of which they very much resent. I mean here by myths not those imageries and mythologies that for instance Lévi-Strauss had in mind, but supposed truths proved in historical writings which are in fact provably untrue but have gained their hold by being comforting to some ascendant political or ethnic structure or to some emotional need. Repetition has anchored them in the mind of the generality. Where would the citizen of the United States be today if he did not grow up with the comforting notion that his country is the one that invented and perfected democracy? As I write this, I recall seeing just today in the press the account of an address by one Francis Fukuyama, once of the Rand Corporation, who thinks that history (by which he means conflict) has come to an end because the whole world has settled into a contented acceptance of the American dream. He foresees an eternity of equilibrium and boredom – all existence a cross between Beverly Hills and Scarsdale. He has a lot to learn, but comes conveniently to hand to prove my point. What would the average Frenchman feel if he could not suppose that his nation had created all the civilization worth having, from literature at one end to furniture and food at the other? What is to become of the Englishman who has had to come to terms with the discovery that the supposedly upward moves of progress and perfection in power, in politics, and in government, which once he believed history told him characterized his country, were also an invention of the dream-makers? It is, after all, the myths put up by historians that have given their subject much of its general attraction.

Yet where do we stand today? Ever since historical study became professional – that is to say, systematic, thorough and grounded in the sources – it has time and again destroyed just those interpretations that served particular interests, more especially national self-esteem and self-confidence. The blatantly jingoistic imperialism of late-

Victorian England quickly succumbed to historical inquests which by the 1930s had removed all unthinking satisfaction with England's imperial past. The conventional view which treated the American War of Independence as a purely idealistic assertion of principle against foreign tyranny has undergone repeated revisions that have left almost none of it standing, at least among the more serious readers of serious history. Some of the myth, interestingly enough, hung on in American public life: thus Franklin Delano Roosevelt's instinctive hostility to the British Empire, which so notably contributed to its disappearance after 1945, owed a good deal to unreconstructed views about the eighteenth century drummed into him in his schooldays. Myths can be danger-ous as well as comforting. The liberal myths which have of late forwarded what is called selfgovernment everywhere – myths which combined noble intentions with a striking ignorance about both past and present – have, since the 1960s, killed far more people in previously imperial terri-tories than 200 years of building those empires ever des-troyed. And they have powerfully assisted the emergence of tyrannies. To the historian the ironies of history have their attraction, but this one seems to me to have gone too far; it is yet another facet of the truth that the world is now in the hands of adolescents.

I am not, of course, suggesting that people must always be able to foresee the consequences of their actions, especially actions based on honest and generous convictions, which is to say myths. Admittedly, it would help if now and again they looked at the sort of history that undermines myths. When it can be shown that such actions, in the past, were misconceived because they in their turn rested on myths about that past's past, the better understanding brought by informed hindsight and sound historical investi-gation should not be shut out of the public mind. Of course, the demolition of comfortable myths causes pain at best and horror-struck revulsion at worst; it can lead to a dangerous over-reaction. The myth of good old Uncle Joe Stalin and the virtues of the Soviet system, carefully put together by commentators in the 1930s and given currency by the circumstances of the last Great War, lay behind many of the errors perpetrated in the settlements of the 1940s. Once historians (some historians) had exploded the myth, far too much policy came to be directed by an equally simple-minded abhorrence and fear. However, that myth seems to be decently killed and buried now that the truth about that murderous regime has been admitted by the Russians themselves, bravely replacing myth by reality in a fashion that we might term exemplary for other nations in their mistaken self-satisfaction; meanwhile, the lesson might still be learned which emerges from the refusal of so many perfectly decent and well educated people in Britain and the United States to believe the manifest truth for some forty years or more. There are times when I feel forced to regard the intellectual community not only with surprise but with horror.

One of the most interesting cases of the myth problem occurred in Germany, the original home of advanced historical science. Since the notable nineteenth-century historians there were nearly all fairly simpleminded patriots, they accepted myths about the medieval empire which they came to treat as the model and paradigm for a Germany reunited in their own day. Thus on the myth they erected interpretations which demanded profound loyalty to the nation and its expansionist state. The myth survived the First World War and played an important role in the rise of Nazism. The Second World War, assisted by new historians, destroyed it, to a point where a wholesale revulsion against the national past seemed to have set in; it has taken thirty years or so for the German educational system to return to an interest, now sober and generally sensible, in that past. Even so, this has been achieved in the main by eliminating the middle ages from the story altogether and, even more impressively, by forgetting Prussia at the speed of light. So far as I can tell, in West Germany, at least, history is unusually free of myths among the consumers, and it will be interesting to see whether this state of affairs can endure. Will there be new myths to absorb an interest in the past and give comfort to the present; or will Germans insist on seeing the past unclouded by myths; or will the death of myth in the end terminate anything like a serious concern with the past? That country looks likely to provide an interesting laboratory experiment.

Normally, myths enjoy tough constitutions, nor should we forget that what overthrows them may in turn partake of the nature of a myth, especially if the historical revision employs a general theory to do its work. The myth of the wonderful and beneficent British Empire was destroyed by historians such as R. H. Tawney who aimed to reconstruct society to a pattern they thought ideal – open, generous, free. Predictably this meant that the history they used to do down what they found was at least as biased, one-sided and indeed erroneous as that which it came to replace, and for some thirty years now some of us have been trying to undo the unfortunate consequences of their idealism. This does not mean restoring the earlier myth, or at least it should not and need not mean that, but the risk exists. When I have attacked Tawney it has been taken for granted that I wished to make party-political points – that I was being as Tory as he was a champion of the Labour Party. But what concerned me was the falsehood of his historical technique and the consequent creation of new myths – especially the myth that seemed to prove that political liberty was bound to be linked to social abuse. I did not, of course, expect to be read correctly by people who are committed emotionally to their myths, but I do think it is the historian's duty to put myths in their place (which is the discard) regardless of what some people may feel about it all. Nobody seems to doubt this when the myths are nasty, as for instance the lies built around the so-called Protocols of the Elders of Zion – though I might draw your attention to the current activities of an English historian, David Irving, who is actively denying the holocaust and accusing Churchill of destroying the British Empire in the service of his own selfish glory. No myth will ever quite die, least of all in a world which believes in the truth of the bible. When it comes to understanding the past, comfortable myths should be no more acceptable than their opposite. Some years ago, Sir John Plumb, aware of the threat both to the general mind and to the survival of his profession that the undermining of ancient convictions could pose, in effect advised historians to write the sort of history that helps people towards a contented and more cheerful life.[13] But surely that is to back corruption: we are not to tell what for good reason we believe to be much nearer the truth if it upsets people. Besides, it cannot be done. All history upsets some people: what Plumb really called for was the sort of history that supported the social attitudes, ambitions and behaviour that he preferred.

No, it is the search for truth that must guide our labours, which is why that attack on the very possibility of discovering a truth of history is so very devastating – leaving aside the fact that it rests upon much ignorance of what seeking that truth actually means. It is only by providing as truthful an understanding of the past as we can obtain that we can offer to the present a past which can be useful to the present, a past from which it can learn. I have preached this gospel often enough, though I do not seem to have converted all that many of my fellow historians. Partly this is because I cannot pretend to bring much comfort, especially in the face of the philosophers and social scientists who question the very notion of a truth in history. They will not accept that it is there, in the events of the past, and open to investigation, even if it will never be recovered in full and beyond all

[13] J. H. Plumb, *The Death of the Past* (London, 1969).

doubt. That uncertainty around historical truth and a true view of the past arises from the deficiencies of the evidence and the problems it poses, rather than from the alleged transformation of events in the organizing mind of the historian. That doctrine, however dressed up, leads straight to a frivolous nihilism which allows any historian to say whatever he likes. We historians are firmly bound by the authority of our sources (and by no other authority, human or divine), nor must we use fiction to fill in the gaps. And though gaps and ambiguities close the road to total reconstruction, the challenges they pose lead to those fruitful exchanges, even controversies, among historians which do as much as anything does to advance our outworks ever nearer to the fortress of truth. That shall be the theme of my last lecture.

3

Some Prescriptions

It brings some comfort to the historian to learn that the sea of troubles in which he finds himself especially in the United States is by no means unprecedented. In the later middle ages, philosophers and theologians had so far refined their analytical techniques that no two people seemed able to agree with one another on any number of the main issues of the faith: confusion reigned as well as mutual abuse and denunciation. Some people, anxious to gain reassurance about their salvation, turned away altogether from what we are now asked to call the intellectual community; they took refuge in a mysticism which renounced reason and encouraged the generality to believe in magic. But the main response among the trained thinkers turned out to be different. From the confusion and excessive subtlety of the schools there emerged what came to be called humanism: a decision to cut the cackle and rediscover essentials. The humanist cry was 'ad fontes', back to the sources; and anyone today who is anxious to restore sense and soundness to history will be well advised to pick up that message.

Anyone who wants to free history from the elastic bonds woven by linguists, literary critics and psychologists (the relativist nominalists of our day) without subjecting it to the arrogant rule of the social scientists (to continue the medieval parallel, the realists on the scene) is likely to find himself despised and denounced as a positivist or historicist, or both; and in the vocabulary of the day there are no more powerful terms of abuse. But the historical past can be studied purposefully, convincingly and successfully (within limits), and it can and does help the present without extruding major interpretative theories. I do not intend to discourse at length about objectivity or about history's independence of the historian because what is real about those concepts can only be experienced by the historian in the course of doing his work – which is why the charges against these truths are always being levelled by people who have not tried to do the real work of history. The simplicities of the faith that inspired a good many nineteenth-century historians, eliciting from them both assertive confidence and often erroneous conclusions, depended on that belief in total objectivity, and it can readily be rejected. But rejection does not mean that one has to move over into an equally assertive confidence derived from the opposite set of false assumptions and breeding erroneous conclusions. No sensible historian would now wish to treat history as a science in the sense that its study produces proven, verifiable and unvarying truths – though the post-Newtonian view of the physical world, denying the absolute, allowing for the unpredictably contingent, and accepting the effect of the observer upon the matter observed might not be a bad analogy for good history. However, the wise historian will not align himself exclusively with either the nominalist or the realist; he will keep away from both Ockham and Aquinas. I shall endeavour to maintain that history should not be regarded as merely a form of some other intellectual enterprise: it has its own operating rules, its own independent function, and its own contribution to make to the intellectual and social life of mankind.

The other concept much derided is that we should study the past for its own sake. This seems often to be read as meaning that we should treat the past as irrelevant to the present, and since one of the reasons for studying the past for its own sake lies in the danger which a present-centred history opposes to the objectivity of the exercise the misunderstanding becomes comprehensible. Nevertheless, it is

a serious and disturbing misunderstanding of the fundamental demand made on the historian, namely that he
should study the past without directing it to any ends chosen
by himself. Studying the past for its own sake means giving
to the past the right to exist within the terms of its own
experience and more especially remembering the freedom of
choice which at one time existed for its agents – the people –
with whom we are dealing. This does not take away the use
of hindsight; of course the historian has to employ his
knowledge of what happened next in order to understand
what happened before. But he must not convert hindsight
into prophecy; he must not declare the after-event to be
totally predictable and leading to those aspects of his own
present that he wishes to promote, nor must he assign
importance only to what happened after. In other words,
studying the past for its own sake means only treating it as
independent of the later day, in the knowledge that only in
this way a true past has a chance to emerge and can then be
related to the present.

We are therefore looking for a way to ground historical
reconstruction in something that offers a measure of
independent security – independent of the historian,
independent of the concerns of his day, independent of the
social and political conditions imposed on him. And the
obvious answer to this quest, as it has always been and must
continue to be, lies in the sources he has at his disposal. *Ad
fontes* remains the necessary war cry. For the historian the
reality – yes, the truth – of the past exists in materials of
various kinds, produced by that past at the time that it
occurred and left behind by it as testimony. Historical
evidence is not created by the historian, and little of it was
deliberately created for him; it is simply that deposit of past
happenings that still exists to be looked at. The philosophical discussions of history and historical evidence have unfortunately concentrated far too much on the sources used by
historians of ideas (or practitioners of intellectual history);

that is to say, they have tried to work out how one can or should use materials created in the past as interpretative vehicles for ideas. As we all know, there is a great deal of historical research and writing that deals with quite other matters and relies on very different source material, which means that the peculiar arguments about the study of 'texts' help hardly at all in our understanding of the tasks undertaken by most historians. On the other hand, however, a case can be made for the recognition and treatment of historical evidence which would embrace all of it, including the writings of political philosophers.

Historical evidence, as I have said, comprehends the extant traces of past events and experiences. If it is to be used it needs to be correctly understood; mere surface or immediate impressions are likely to be inadequate. The correct reading of historical evidence requires at least a measure of training, of professional skills properly acquired and applied, and although this fact may be more obvious when the past in question is a long distance away it remains true also for the supposedly familiar territory of recent history. It is here that I must take issue with Professor Theodore Hamerow who recently expressed regret at what he called 'the bureaucratization of history'.[1] While he agreed that the manner in which historical enterprises had, in the last century, become professionalized deserved serious respect, he held that too much had been lost, and for this he blamed the straitjackets imposed by organization in institutions. He felt that formal graduate instruction demanded far too rigorous a form of behaviour, and he thought that overcautious specialization had produced a real fragmentation of the work, with those professionalized practitioners concentrating ever more exclusively on their own little bits from the human past. In consequence, he maintained, historians had ceased to address the general public and had become pedan-

---

[1] *American Historical Review* 94/3 (1989), 654–60.

tic, inward-looking and uninteresting. Now I have no doubt that all these bad things can happen to the products of American graduate schools, and I am aware that pedantry always lies in wait everywhere to strangle scholarship. But look at the alternative. The major escape routes would seem to be signposted by the obtrusive theoreticians, especially the prophets of uncertainty, relativism and individual self-love, to the point where history is said to have no independent reality at all. It is this nihilist conclusion that a proper training – a professional training – in the treatment of the historical evidence will eliminate: real and informed contact with the relics of the past ought to cure people of those philosophical vapours. Of course, professional training of the kind I speak of is only the beginning of the enterprise. If nothing more were to emerge from that start than the sort of bureaucratically controlled specialization that Hamerow has in mind, history would indeed soon lose its claim to attention. But in the first place, if the work is to be soundly based and to deserve even modified credence, it has to rest upon the sort of inside understanding which only professional attitudes and training can supply.

Let me explain what I mean. Historians, as I have said, reconstruct some part and aspect of the past out of the relics which that past has left behind and which we call historical evidence. It includes everything that came into existence at the time studied and is still in existence at the time that study takes place. It therefore includes, obviously, writings of that day whether they be chronicles or sermons or treatises; it includes letters and memoranda; it includes records produced in legal processes or the running of affairs both great and small. There are orders by agencies of rule and reactions to such orders; financial accounts; last wills and testaments; analyses of landed estates and merchants' dealing; and so forth. But it also includes unwritten survivals, whether they be town walls, field systems, artefacts and coins, again and so forth. The use of this motley collection of relics will naturally vary according to the questions put to it, but the one thing that unites them as a category – the fact that they constitute the positive bequest left by the past to the present – also poses the fundamental problem, which is the same for them all. Those relics have to be correctly understood, which is not at all the same thing as being processed through the historian's personal mind. If the material is to be correctly understood we must always start from one basic question: how and why did it come into existence? The purposes served by the human beings who first created it, and the manner of their proceeding in so creating it, are the ways into a proper understanding of the historical evidence, which is to say that the fundamental questions we put to the evidence are independent of the concerns of the questioner and focused entirely on the concerns of the original creators.

A few examples will show what I have in mind. I have often been charged with a preoccupation with administrative technicalities, a supposedly arid field of study loudly despised by those who seek the deeper realities of social analysis. But the documents upon which the social historian relies were as a rule the product of administrative processes, and unless those processes are understood the products will be misjudged and misused. If not all that many historians take the technical details of legal records at face value it is unfortunately more often because they are scared of them and would rather not use them at all than master their technical inwardness. Le Roy Ladurie could treat denunciations collected in a visitation as though they described proven behaviour in the Cathar village of Montaillou. Even so, accusations of treasonable acts sent to Thomas Cromwell were regularly treated as proof of tyrannous oppression, until I ventured to ask the question what happened to the charges contained in those letters. When I tried to follow the process of investigation, possibly leading to trials and condemnations, the exercise (which was reasonably tedious to undertake and seems to have bored a few readers whose preconceptions were at stake) demonstrated that the government of Henry VIII took care to ascertain the truth in those denunciations; only if there was substance in them did the government follow things up in accordance with the facts and the law in force.[2] I once made myself fairly unpopular in some quarters when I discussed the current interest in the history of crime and had to point out that the historians in question had little idea of how the people they were discussing classified offences or what processes they used to prosecute offenders. Yet on those technical details depended the meaning of the documents they were using. Historians of England who use the records of the law before the nineteenth century have to come to terms with the fact that it was only in that century that law came to be seen in the modern fashion as a reflection of changing social attitudes; before that it was regarded as absolute and standing apart from the effects upon those who made and used it. Of course, in so treating it past ages often deceived themselves, but self-deception is an important aspect of the problem and is reflected in the manner in which the evidence came into existence.

Ignorance of the technical details – administrative details, if you like – can lead to error which at first looks small but often has wide repercussions. I have known scholars who tried to see significance in the forms of address used in letters from the kings of England in the medieval and early-modern periods. Some people were called 'trusty and well beloved', others 'right trusty and well beloved', and some got no such adjectives at all. It has proved easy to assume that those differences described differing relationships with political significance. In actual fact, they signify only differences in the social standing of the recipients and are purely formal. A familiar example of this kind of misunderstanding deserves

[2] G. R. Elton, *Policy and Police: The Enforcement of the Reformation in the Age of Thomas Cromwell* (Cambridge, 1972).

citing again because it comprehensively illustrates the vital need to read the materials of historical evidence as the products of an ascertainable process. Studying the history of Parliament, the eminent Tudor historian A. F. Pollard some eighty years ago found letters under the great seal enrolled on the Patent Roll with the annotation 'datum de mandatu Parliamenti'. Translating this, understandably enough, as 'given by order of the Parliament', he concluded that in the fifteenth century grants ostensibly made by the Crown were regularly authorized by or in Parliament, an institution which thus at one fell swoop acquired widespread influence in the government of England. But what the phrase really meant was 'dated by the authority of Parliament' – a reference to the parliamentary statute of 1439 (18 Henry VI, c. 1) which laid it down that the date of letters under the great seal should be the date on which the warrants for them were delivered into the Chancery, the office responsible for issuing them. The act did not give Parliament any power to intervene in the making of grants; it was solely designed to prevent fraudulent predating or oppressive delays in dating by limiting the Chancery's freedom to put a date on the document. If Pollard had looked at the warrants for those instruments he would have found written at the top of each of them the words 'deliberatum domino cancellario in Cancellaria regis' (delivered to the lord chancellor in the king's Chancery) on a day stated, that day then, under the statute ('de mandatu Parliamenti'), becoming the date of the great seal patent made in response to the warrant. The use of documents produced by any administrative machine is beset by dangers of this sort, dangers which only a proper understanding of the how and why involved in the document's creation can overcome. And it is the task of the specialist training imposed on the budding historian to bring about that understanding.

A very different example. Philippe Ariès wrote some highly influential books on childhood in the middle ages and beyond. One of his major conclusions maintained that not until the eighteenth century did Europeans begin to treat childhood as a particular stage in the human being's development and as clearly separate from adulthood. One of his chief arguments for this erroneous opinion was that before that time paintings of children showed them dressed in miniaturized versions of grown-up clothes. There are quite a few objections to his views anyway, but what matters here is that Ariès ignored, or failed to know, that when parents had their children painted they naturally dressed them up in their finery; ordinarily they were hardly ever seen in the appearance they put on in those pictures. Ordinarily they looked like children, not like small adults. Thus the clinching argument used by Ariès to support a conclusion otherwise largely derived from a refusal to search out the evidence depended on a plain failure to grasp how the evidence he did use came into existence. And considerable edifices were erected in his wake by historians anxious to prove that European parents had no affection for their children.

In this basic task of really understanding the evidence a great many skills and much penetration need to be applied; it is folly to denigrate or doubt the importance of the stage which transforms the relics of the past into usable evidence for the reality of the past. The theorists we have been fighting off like to play with the historical material as though they were in charge of it; they like to think either that they are its master or that all treatment is so uncontrolled that there cannot be any ascertainable certainties in history. Professor Himmelfarb a little while ago drew attention to one self-confident historian, one Dr Dominic La Capra, who warned historians against becoming what he was pleased to call 'fact-fetishistic'.[3] True, if one wants to play silly games with

---

[3] Compare Gertrude Himmelfarb, 'Some Reflections on the New History', *American Historical Review* 94/3 (1989), 661–70. Dominic La Capra has developed his curiously vapoury notions in *History and Criticism* (Ithaca, 1983); he is dealt with quite faithfully by Peter Novick, *That Noble Dream* (Cambridge, 1989), 603–5.

history it is best to deny the existence of facts. To La Capra, everything about the past is indeterminate, including even well-established dates – on the remarkable grounds that various ages have used different chronological systems. Thus our conventional dating before and after the birth of Christ becomes merely an observer's construct. This (I fear) is a classic example of the mindless arrogance of the self-satisfied operator. The dating of past events is, of course, basic to any acceptable reconstruction of the historical scene, and there is not the slightest doubt that such events occurred on definable occasions within the flow of time. The historian's task here consists in establishing the date. He may find it expressed in terms of a chronological scale that differs from his own and therefore needs converting: it may rely on the ancient Roman, or the Jewish, or the Muslim dating system, for instance. That fact, however, does not alter its place in time which also is in no way altered by his transcribing the date into the system with which he operates. The moment of occurrence remains untouched – and remains completely independent of the operating intelligence. The same absence of indeterminacy incidentally also applies if the date cannot be established.

The contempt expressed by some who claim to be historians for the basic duty to establish the true origin of the historical evidence must come as a surprise to anybody who has not encountered the strange gyrations of people affected by false philosophies. I have, of course, tried to preach my cause before this; I have written about the existence of historical evidence independently of the historian, and of the nature of the tasks facing him in gaining comprehension before he uses it. Dr La Capra, whom I have just had occasion to mention, took courteous exception to my arguments; he maintains that what I have said may apply to documents but is of no relevance to the historian of ideas who uses 'texts'.[4]

---

[4] La Capra, *History and Criticism*, 136–8.

What he calls my 'model of knowledge' he declares to be 'necessary but not sufficient for historical research', and it will not suffice 'in a field such as intellectual history'. I am accused of believing that historical treatment must be either objective or relativist, whereas there is a third way, though what it may be does not become clear. Some of his sayings are too arcane for me: thus he seeks to investigate 'many aspects of cognitively responsible but still responsive exchange between past and present', which seems to hint once again that what matters is the investigating historian and not the investigated past. But the real answer to Dr La Capra cuts more deeply. He used my book as he uses his alleged 'texts', applying his critical techniques to it, and in the process he manufactured a remarkable assembly of tendentious misinterpretations, including the charge that when I hoped that the historian might at times be able to tell a story I demanded that all historians should always aim at constructing nothing but narratives. What all his argument proves – somewhat, I admit, to my satisfaction – is that a method which ostentatiously perverts the sense of a minor twentieth-century manual need not be expected to do anything useful with the intellectual history of mankind.

The error here lies first and foremost in the failure to realize that the sources used by the historian of ideas are like all other historical sources inasmuch as they were produced in the past, survive into the present, and require instructed analysis before they can be understood and used. And that analysis must rest on historical principles, not on the methods developed for the study of literary materials by critics even further removed from real life. The specific techniques involved in understanding them may well be peculiar to themselves, even as the techniques for correctly understanding private letters differ markedly from those needed to comprehend legal proceedings or archaeological finds. Yet the same basic rules – the questions how and why they came into existence – apply to them all equally. It is certainly true that endless debates have revolved around the methods supposedly needed to unlock the secrets of those particular sources, mainly because so many people studying them would like to remove them from the particulars of history into a heaven of philosophy. But all that means is that how they are to be understood remains in doubt, as it often does for other documents; it does not mean that they differ fundamentally from all the other historical evidence, from the material which La Capra writes off as documents. I have to confess that his example does not encourage trust in the evanescent methods of the literary critic, methods specifically designed not to clarify the meaning of past creations but to give first place to the present-day observer pandering to his soul. The trouble seems to be that literary and critical theory so readily absolves the operator from reading what is actually in the text he is supposedly study-ing. Thus another critic of my *Practice of History* cites me as saying that 'books should differ with the people to whom they are addressed', without noticing that a few lines further on I declare that often proclaimed advice to be 'wrong-headed and rather pernicious'.[5] There is, I fear, no substitute for hard and careful work on the sources, respecting them but seeking really to understand them, and this applies in the history of ideas quite as much as in any other historical enterprise.

If I seem to labour this point it is, I fear, because what working historians tend to know well enough is not so obvious to the commentators who have little or no experi-ence of working with historical materials. And unfortu-nately, expert skills in most other intellectual exercises offer at most a tiny bit of help to historians. The typical mental processes of the philosopher or the critic or the social

---

[5] Lionel Gossman, 'History and Literature', in *The Writing of History*, ed. Robert H. Canary and Henry Kosicki (Madison, 1978), 3–39; see esp. p. 39. Compare G. R. Elton, *The Practice of History* (Sydney, 1967), 115.

scientist, no matter to what school they may belong, are essentially hostile to the typical (and necessary) mental processes of the historian. And this brings me to the nub of the issue. There is such a thing as the historical method – a set of rules and principles that describe the work done by the historian – which differs from the rules and principles worked out for and by other intellectual disciplines. Therefore the introduction of alien devices, contrary to what some people seem to think, operates against historical understanding and reconstruction rather than assisting it. The logician seeks order and, following Ockham, wishes to reduce the multiplicity of any phenomenon to a formal simplicity elevating some aspects to the exclusion of others; historians who would so treat their sources would rightly be accused of reductionism – of emphasizing this or that aspect by neglecting others that do not fit the scheme. The philosopher wishes to subsume the confusion of reality under general guiding principles which offer an explanation applicable to any set of discoverable phenomena; the historian allows for the constant accretion of detail that disrupts premature or even ultimate structures. The physicist – perhaps the natural scientist in general – also seeks (as Thomas Kuhn explained decades ago) to establish paradigmatic constructs which both govern the course of the enquiry and make comprehensible sense of its outcome; the historian operates mainly by subjecting every paradigm on offer to a sceptical questioning in the light of discoverable detail. The student, and especially the producer, of literature, be it prose or verse, is engaged in putting forward constructions informed by his imagination and free will; the historian is not allowed to invent convenient detail to make a convincing story and, confronted by his evidence, has very little free will. Take the old and really rather dead debate whether history is a science or an art: in any precise sense it is neither. For it cannot expect to arrive at knowledge testable by falsification or verification (the secret of a science), nor can it manipulate its subject matter so as to produce morally or aesthetically satisfying results (the characteristic of an art). In short, history is a study different from any other and governed by rules peculiar to itself.

This is not to say that the methods, and up to a point the products, of other forms of enquiry are totally irrelevant to the historian. The subject matter of history is human beings – their experiences, actions, thought and sufferings – but human beings in the past. It follows then that all the various ways in which human beings have tried to understand themselves have something to say to the historian. Psychology, anthropology, sociology, folklore, criticism of art and literature, all these and any other forms of study that you can think of do concern the study of History, subject to one condition: their processes and products must be subjected to the historical treatment in the same way as past politics, say, or economics have been, topics once the primary areas of historical interest. They are in exactly the same position as are traditional schemes of ideas commonly used in historical analysis, such as theology or law or military science. While it is necessary to know what their practitioners are talking about, it matters that such knowledge is the beginning and not the outcome of historical enquiry. Trouble arises if the methods of those other intellectual enterprises are allowed to take charge, so that the past is despised and explained simply under the guidance of current forms of enquiry. The real usefulness of those other studies, I would maintain, lies not in the provision of answers but exclusively in the posing of questions: grasping what an anthropologist or psychologist puts forward does not answer a single question about the past but may suggest lines of enquiry not previously pursued. In all work on the past the historical method, employing a great variety of techniques, must control if the result is to be trustworthy.

Working historians are no strangers to this problem. Thus that eminent legal historian, Raoul van Caenegem, encountered it when he tried to work out why in the course of the twelfth century the law of England took so different a course from that of the continent.[6] He reviewed some of the causes previously alleged – the notion that 'the English' were a people marked by a discoverable national character, the concept of a set of characteristics (in science, religion, law and so forth) all reducible to a common and particular quality in the nation, or perhaps that frequent refuge, the economic factor. None of this, he explained, got him any forrarder in his search. 'Let us therefore,' he continued, 'give up this sociologist's chase for some general factor and do the proper work of the historian by studying the precise and particular circumstances in which the common law arose, without forgetting that some were not less important because they were fortuitous.' The last phrase needs underlining. Historical analysis does not attempt to extract some general or overriding cause from a welter of circumstances: it allows for them all. Having shunted aside the sociologist, van Caenegem then proceeded to answer his question most satisfactorily in an argument extending over some twenty pages, neglecting nothing, clarifying everything and highlighting major points by analysis, not by assertion or by obedience to a general theory.

What, then, is the fundamental character of that historical method – allowing for the fact that different periods of the past and different questions asked of it call for the application of different techniques under the general aegis of that method? The method has been developed in response to the special problems posed by the desire to understand human experiences which unquestionably occurred at some time in the past but are now traceable only through such bits and pieces of evidence as the past had left behind. The work is thus governed by certain inescapable conditions. Reality has to be rediscovered and described on the basis of know-

[6] Raoul van Caenegem, *The Birth of the English Common Law* (Cambridge, 1973), 85–110.

ledge which is invariably incomplete, often highly ambiguous, and cannot be enlarged once all the relevant survivals have been studied, all of which demands constant decisions based on choice among the possibilities. That choice, however, must be exercised not on the ground of views and explanations contemporary with the historian; the present must be kept out of the past if the search for the truth of that past is to move towards such success as in the circumstances is possible. That partial and uneven evidence must be read in the context of the day that produced it; reading it must never be governed by any desire to justify or explain or even just to understand the present. The worst of all methods is one that I would call dogmatic: it uses past evidence selectively to underpin answers previously arrived at. I discussed that form of corruption in my first lecture. The next worst method reads the evidence under the general instruction of some critical or philosophical theory put up today (and usually soon replaced by another such clever device): that confusion I dealt with in my second lecture. I repeat, nor can I say it often enough: if we seek such truth as historical enquiry is capable of finding we must study the past for its own sake and guided by its own thoughts and practices.

The operation, difficult enough in itself, is made more so by the only means that enables us to initiate it at all. That means is hindsight. Working on history means working on what is gone, even if the distance it has gone is only a short one. (Usually, of course, it is pretty long.) Therefore, inevitably, we know what happened next, and the risk is always considerable that the historian will fall victim to the false old proposition, *post hoc ergo propter hoc*, the succeeding event being read as a necessary consequence of the earlier event. At once we are in the toils of predictability, in an extreme case even of predestination. And yet we neither can escape hindsight nor can we do without it, because only a knowledge of what came next draws attention to a given bit of the past as demanding treatment. In part, of course, the problems posed by hindsight are similar to those posed by the patchy and ambiguous character of historical evidence: all these defects limit the degree of certainty possible in historical reconstruction. But this should matter hardly at all, once we have come to accept so basic a fact about the historian's existence. He must from the beginning understand and accept that all he says will lack the perfection of proof, will be subject to review and perhaps attack, and will constitute part of an ever continuing dialogue. If he does his work well he can also rest assured that much of his reconstruction will stand up to future tests and that even errors and slips will almost certainly, by the correction they provoke, contribute to an improvement in understanding. Everything, therefore, depends on what one means by the phrase, 'if he does his work well', and there certainly exist differences of opinion on that point. I can only state my principles, though I can claim that they are principles which I have seen employed successfully by myself and by others. Nor are they very obscure, and they do not need to hide behind pseudo-intellectual jargon.

The first principle reads: separate your question from your answer. By this I mean no more than that the question one puts to the evidence should not be biased towards an answer already in the mind. And this means that in the first place one solicits questions from the evidence. It is wrong to start with exact questions carrying built-in answers. For example it is wrong to investigate the English civil wars of the seventeenth century by asking what social classes the parties represented. To ask this simply assumes a meaningful relationship between class and choice of side. The right question might read: can I find any characteristics that distinguished members of the two sides from each other? As it happens, the first discovery in this instance would show that the participants of the war came on both sides from much the same social strata, so that the class-based explanation, so widely used, would at once have to be abandoned as wrong, but if the enquirer had assumed that differences in class mattered he would (as he has often done) soon construct a misleading set of proofs. Under the guidance of the right question, other parts of the profile would assume greater significance, such perhaps as relative age, certainly geographical location, placement within the faction structure of the royal court, very probably religion and ideologies. The real and complex picture would emerge by stages, with none of the answers derived from questions expressly beamed at them and then elicited by evidence suitably picked from the mass.

The second principle says: remember that you have the advantage and burden of hindsight, whereas the people you are talking about lacked this. This is one of the essential points in what I have called studying the past on its own terms, with proper respect for it and its inhabitants. This does involve the subjection of the historian's self to the object of his study. True, it may not be an easy thing to achieve, but that seems to me no reason for not trying for it. I remember that when I was younger I was often accused of judging the Tudor century by the standards and criteria which it itself employed, and I frankly cannot think of a more flattering comment. With this second principle there disappears one of the most pernicious commonplaces of the contemporary analysis of historical labours, namely that what the historian will say is dominated by his personality — by the alleged opinions and prejudices which others claim to discern in him. It is not true that every generation rewrites history in its own image; rather, it is as possible as it is necessary to minimize, even to eliminate, the effects of the historian's personal preferences and attitudes upon the work done. The idea has gained so much ground because it excuses mere bigoted idleness in the operator and elevates his own personal concerns to a position of first importance in his work. One of the most striking examples of this form of corruption is found among the more strident feminist historians. Any historian is fully entitled to hold views about women and men, about patriarchy and gender relationships and all the other preoccupations of her own day, but she is most certainly not entitled to measure people in the past by standards worked out in the present. To treat the women of the past as miserable deviants from the truths of the sisterhood – truths they had never heard of – is very wrong, and the more so because the chief purpose of such history is to shore up the uneasy feeling that what now passes for truth may also be no more than an accident of time. Inasmuch as it is true that historians cannot altogether escape from infusing themselves into their work, they should remain constantly aware of the danger and provide remedy, rather than surrender to it and be proud of the admission.

The third and last general principle that I would propose says this: keep an open mind. Allow further study and fuller knowledge, whether it comes from your own work or that of others, to modify what you have thought and said. In an intellectual enterprise which can never reach a total and totally agreed consummation, this may sound like preaching the obvious, but at times the obvious needs most preaching. We all tend to get committed to our reconstructions and, having extracted them from the evidence by the use of all the proper methods, hard work and (we hope) mental flexibility, find it burdensome when they are contradicted, perhaps disproved. Well, it happens, and the historian had better be ready for it. Unfortunately, such readiness can express itself in an unwillingness ever to make positive statements, a predilection for covering one's tracks in arcane verbiage and ambiguity, an inclination to write badly because to write well leads to a risk of contest and contradiction. Too many historians have used the thickets of obscure language to take cover while casting apprehensive looks at others.

However, all that this means is that all those basic principles, which it is the function of a professional training to instil in the historian, are hard to observe. Writing history correctly is a very difficult task, just because the subject matter is so enormous, lends itself so readily to partial and partisan treatment, and will, improperly treated, provide the appearance of proof for any answer. To cope with such problems is much more testing than to practise research in the sciences which reduce their subject matters to essentials and can rest positive conclusions upon them. This the historian cannot and must not do, for which reason his labours will always seem exceptionally hard and his results exceptionally provisional. But we have our compensation: none of our areas of study ever dies on us.

This, however, must raise the last question that I mean to discuss today. If history spreads before us all the traps and pitfalls I have listed, why do we study it at all? What do we hope to achieve by offering our tentative and incomplete reconstructions of a past that has been and gone? That many people find pleasure and satisfaction in these endeavours is not a sufficient answer; after all, the same is true of sex murderers. It is certainly the case, and an important one, that the historian acts as the keeper of humanity's memory. The ability to recall past experience is one of the special attributes of the human species, an attribute which equips it with a three-dimensional view of life and enables it to think beyond the immediate needs of the body. It also burdens mankind with that troublesome memory that diminishes the easy and thoughtless life of the child, but then all the things that distinguish men and women from other forms of creation are both a necessary joy and an inescapable threat. In any case we cannot escape having a memory, and thus we rely on the historian to order and explain the collective memory within which our individual ability to remember, and to learn about what we had forgotten, finds its resting place.

In these respects, historians serve all humanity, or rather they should so serve it. Nowadays, caught in the toils of a self-conscious professionalism, they too often evade that duty, leaving the task of telling about the past to the untrained and largely ignorant – to the writers of fiction, avowed or disguised, to the makers of films, to the journalists and speculators of the pen. I am puzzled to know why so much good history is so evilly presented, in language deliberately clumsy and obscure. There was a time, about two generations ago, when leading historians (especially of the middle ages) sneered at any colleague who could be read without agony and boredom as manifestly not serious in his occupation: if he could be understood by people outside the ranks of the mystery he was clearly not talking about the complexities of the real past. This silly attitude after a bit began to dissipate, and practitioners of other disciplines – especially sociology and political science – moved in to take over the deserted mansions of jargon and pretentiousness. But alas, historians, especially in France and the United States, allowed themselves to be persuaded once again that real intellectual quality cannot co-exist with plain language, clear expression and a non-technical vocabulary. First the social sciences and a little later the mysteries of critical theory began to corrupt the historian's speech. Unreal constructs like elite, gender groups, peer groups, structural and poststructural analysis, crept in side by side with the dead terms of ancient rhetoric (metonymy, you will remember, or synecdoche) in a quite unnecessary endeavour to dress the work in borrowed plumes. On this contentious point I must state my plain conviction. When the historian has to cope with subject matter that depends on a technical vocabulary he will of necessity have to use and understand that. You cannot talk about the common law without bringing in original writs; about religious conflict without mentioning the sacraments; about early-modern warfare without explaining musketry and pike-drill. But the flow of language within which those necessary technicalities occur must be simple, even ordinary, devoid of pompous obscurity. One of the chief tests of the quality of historical work lies in its readability. History, even serious history, is interesting, and the historian who makes it dull deserves the pillory. One of the few benefits that advancing years bring to the historian is an increasing right to refuse being bored by his colleagues.

However, there is a much more serious reason for demanding that historians should be able to communicate with people in general, a demand which rates clarity of thought and exposition well above that strangely desperate effort to seek the approval of philosophical guides and intellectual despots using secret languages of their own. That reason is found in what in the end must be the role the historian plays in the fortunes of mankind: his standing within his own time and place. I think I have sufficiently denounced the idea that the historian should have the present in mind when investigating the past, but that does not entail ignoring the present altogether. The study of the past must be conducted in its own right so that those who wish to learn from the past can be sure that what is offered has not been shaped to suit some supposed purpose of theirs, or indeed the purposes of the scholar who is giving them access to it.

What really matters here is the meaning of that dangerous little phrase, learning from the past. A good many people seem to suppose that a sound understanding of history will give direct guidance for present action. Know how things have come to be as they are, and you will know what to do next. Yet attitudes shaped by past experience often offer quite misleading instructions to those who hold them. Take a case, a big case, of considerable relevance today. Owing to two World Wars largely unleashed by imperialist ambitions entertained by successive German governments, it is now widely felt that the resurgence of Germany once again threatens the peace of the world. But when, in 1870, Germany was united under the leadership of that (nowadays) notoriously warlike country, Prussia, the common reaction was very different. That event came after some two centuries of almost uninterrupted aggression by France, and it came as the result of a victorious war against that established disturber of the peace. Therefore, at the time and for some time afterwards, the unification of Germany was very widely regarded (outside France) as a most fortunate event, and Bismarck, later converted into a menace, received much praise and admiration. Attitudes were also much influenced by romantic visions of a romantic Germany. The simple idea that knowledge of what had happened told one what now to expect and to approve sadly misled a lot of well-meaning people. I cannot say whether the revival of Germany now will lead to a revival of German aggression, even though the world's experience between 1914 and 1945 might suggest that it will. It may or it may not – a useless conclusion but one characteristic of what happens when the idea of learning from history is employed in its usual and simple form.

Nevertheless, that idea hides within itself a true and useful meaning. Human beings learn primarily from experience; if they are to think and act profitably – with positive and useful results – they need as wide a vision of the possibilities contained in any given situation and any present assembly of other human beings as they can acquire. An individual experience, of course, is always limited and commonly distorted by prejudice and self-interest: what men and women need is an enlarged experience against which to measure the effect of those disadvantages. That experience is made available by the historian presenting the past in all its variety and potential, and all of it divorced from the immediate needs and concerns of the present. History provides the laboratory in which human experience is analysed, distilled and bottled for use. The so-called lessons of history do not teach you to do this or that now; they teach you to think more deeply, more completely, and on the basis of an enormously enlarged experience about what it may be possible or desirable to do now. One of the most useful lessons so taught precisely contradicts what predicting historians would like to extract from our labours. Instead of telling us that certain conditions can be shown, from past experience, to lead to certain assured consequences, history for ever demonstrates the unexpectedness of the event and so instils a proper scepticism in the face of all those vast and universal claims. A knowledge of the past should arm a man against surrendering to the panaceas peddled by too many myth-makers. This is known as growing up – outgrowing the arrogance of adolescence which, guided by moral principles unchecked by experience, will impose on suffering mankind the solution promoted by ignorance joined to faith. By enormously enlarging personal experience, history can help us to grow up – to resist those who, with good will or ill, would force us all into the straitjackets of their supposed answers to the problems of existence. Thus I will burden the historian with preserving human freedom, freedom of thought and freedom of action, a burden he bears because he knows what happened before when supposedly inescapable schemes of thought and action were forced upon people.

Understand the past in its own terms and convey it to the present in terms designed to be comprehended. And then ask those willing to listen to attend to the real lessons of the past, the lessons which teach us to behave as adults, experienced in the ways of the world, balanced in judgement, and sceptical in the face of all the miracle-mongers.

The Future of the Past:
Inaugural Lecture as Professor of
English Constitutional History
in the University of Cambridge,
1968

MR VICE-CHANCELLOR, LADIES AND GENTLEMEN,

I don't entirely know what inaugural lectures are for. I do not know exactly what it is one inaugurates; and I have given some thought to the matter because it is customary, and I think nicely customary, to produce such an inauguration. It is not that I lecture for the first time, either in this University or in this room. It is a matter of record. I have a press photograph to prove it. It is not the case that the subject of Constitutional History is new in this University. On the contrary. Its ancestry is immense and the best there is in the historical field in Cambridge. I think all history professors in the last fifty years who inaugurated themselves from this desk or any other have paid their tribute to Frederic William Maitland, and I will do so, too, sincerely and with delight. As I have thought for many years, to speak in the University in which Maitland practised is a distinction which for the historian nothing else can entirely equal. And the tradition continued. We are in a sense today called upon to mourn one of our most eminent practitioners, Miss Helen Cam. To succeed somewhere along the line where she stood is once again an honour, a great honour. And the tradition still

This lecture was delivered without a script and with very few notes. Since a man should once in a while show himself willing to stand by his rashnesses and extravagances, I have left the taped record alone, except that in a few places I have mended the grammar and choice of words. One result of the extempore method is that one tends to omit things that one meant to say, and I have therefore added some footnotes by way of explanation, elaboration or correction.

continues. I see before me one of its most eminent members whom I am very glad indeed to see present here. I am only sorry to think that we shall not hear him speak from this platform again, unless we can persuade him otherwise, some day.

So what is it that I am inaugurating? I am inaugurating a chair, a professorship, and it is a peculiar one. There is no progeny, but on the other hand there is also no ancestry, and in consequence there is for once something to inaugurate. I am trying today to put before you what I believe to be the purposes to which I have been called by the University, another most honourable thing of which I am thoroughly conscious – I don't think I've ever been quite so nervous about a lecture before as about this one. The chair is the chair of English Constitutional History. Now I chose that title myself, and I don't think I could have chosen worse, could I? I damned myself twice over. English Constitutional History, in the present climate of opinion. *One* adjective might have been forgiven. Perhaps Chinese Constitutional History would have been all right. Perhaps English Social History would have been wonderful. But no, I will pick them both: English Constitutional History. A defence is necessary, an assertion of the justness of this subject; its survival value is still existent despite all that may be said, and not only thanks to the high flown examination syllabuses of ancient and new universities. And when I came to think about the question how one would justify English Constitutional History and its presence among us still, I began to realize that what I would really have to justify is the continued practice of the study and teaching of history altogether. Why are we in fact still studying and teaching history? What should we be doing? Why should the future be concerned about the past?

Now there are all sorts of debates on this, and all sorts of answers, and I do not pretend that today I shall say anything very novel. For one thing, I am under friendly instruction not to be belligerent.[1] I do not propose to say anything very much about the social sciences, and all those other things that we have discussed often enough before. Enough passion has been poured out about that. This is going to be eirenic – or as eirenic as I can make it, because I shall not know until the end whether peace has been preserved.

We hear a great deal today about the dangers to historical studies, about the death of history, the end of it. This is a new world. A new technology is transforming all. The future must rid itself of its past, and historians are greatly worried by this kind of talk; they are necessarily practitioners of the past; the past is all that matters to them, or all that matters to them professionally, and, if the past is to be written out of the story, what will there be for them, will there be no more historians? The dangers are often seen, I think, in two particular fields or lines. On the one hand there is a general danger: the world will no longer concern itself with its history. On the other there is an academic danger: undergraduates will read another subject. I think both these dangers are at any rate greatly exaggerated, and the first one certainly doesn't exist. There is absolutely no justification in supposing that the world at large is not concerned about history, and I am not now talking about the splendid sales of individual books or the massive production that runs off the presses of history of one kind or another – I am talking about attitudes, I am talking about the way people think about the world. I am concerned solely with the fact that the world is dominated by its history – all the world.

Well, of course, we know that this is necessarily so, but the striking thing, you know, is that it doesn't apply universally. Those who are really dominated by the past are the revolutionaries. Not the conservatives but the revolutionaries. We all know how often it is said that the

---

[1] In a letter from George Kitson Clark.

Russians had their revolution, look, they're still the same Russians – I think that is true.[2] The same is true of the Chinese; and all the real revolutionary events of the past and the present result merely in the continuation of the past, because they are quite excessively aware of the past. This came to me recently very powerfully in the debates and discussions which have occurred on the decline of the Empire and Commonwealth. Those of us who have attended the obsequies of that interesting institution ought to have been struck by one very curious phenomenon. The people who attacked the remnants of imperial splendour (as they would put it) talked in extraordinarily ancient language. When I listened to Mr Michael Foot I seemed to hear Mr John Bright attacking the aristocracy; I seemed to hear men brought up in the days of J. A. Hobson; men still battling the enemy, and the enemy is Cecil Rhodes. There is nothing here but a working off of grudges so ancient, of feelings so antediluvian that the manner in which the past dominates the revolutionaries seems to me to be very apparent indeed. This isn't true of conservatives because conservatives don't *think* about the past at all. The essence of all history is change, and those who resist or deny change are therefore unhistorical; and to want to stay where you are is not a historical attitude, it is a form of idleness, laziness or a recognition that every move is only going to lead to trouble anyway. I'm not denying the virtues of conservatism, you appreciate. I am merely denying that it is dominated by history, by the historical past. That is the preserve of the

---

[2] I had in mind the well established fact that revolutions change much less of the reality of a situation than of its surface appearance, and that they do so because the revolutions think of themselves as the products of historical 'forces'. This excessive awareness of the past, in which seeming rejection really hides loving involvement, results in the speedy readoption of familiar systems and methods: different people but the same old story. The three well attested revolutions of modern Europe – the English, French and Russian – all demonstrate the inability of revolutions to eliminate the past.

left, that is the preserve of the revolutionaries, and as long as this is a revolutionary age the past will be firmly with us, and the world at large will have no difficulty in remembering history . . . wrongly no doubt, falsely perhaps, foolishly perhaps . . . but it will certainly live in its past.[3]

This varies in countries. There is one reason why I am to some extent perhaps entitled to make the double error of naming my chair after England and the Constitution. At least I can claim that I cannot be dominated solely by an unthinking patriotism – a remnant of school-day memories or something like that – which puts England at the centre of everything. I have had some experience of other countries and other opinions. Now one of the most curious things, I think, about the English (if I may for a moment stand aside) is that they suppose themselves to be conscious of history and enveloped in history. They are not. They are both ignorant and indifferent as far as history is concerned. If you want a really historically conscious country, you have to go either to central Europe where they invented their histories in the nineteenth century, manufactured them out of a variety of largely illusory remnants of the past, under the guidance of Herder; or you want to go to the United States where they have so little history that they preserve every little detail with a most devout mind. If you want to find a battle site in England, you cannot. And there have been

---

[3] I should have emphasized that this is particularly true of the English historiographical tradition. English historians have in the main been 'progressive' – whig, liberal, radical, socialist. The occasional conservative among them – an Oman or a Marriott – was clearly so devoid of a mind that he contributed nothing to the tradition, and the violence provoked by Namier owed much to the astonishment felt in conventional circles at the uncalled-for appearance of a historian with tory predilections who clearly outranked the liberals intellectually. The liberal tradition – sometimes right, sometimes wrong; sometimes wise, sometimes bigoted – is so powerful that as a rule it imposes itself also on those who in parliamentary elections vote for the Conservative Party.

battles in England. If you want to find a battle site in Scotland you can only find those in which the Scots were victorious. But if you want to find a battle site in America you find them all, carefully marked, signposted virtually from the New York docks onwards.[4] In this country history is not very present, and it is our task up to a point to make it more present, to make it more available; to make people realize not that the past is a burden, something to be shed, or an amusing, quaint, attractive game, or something which you sell brick by brick to Hollywood; but that the past is quite simply the matrix in which we live and from which we grow, which utterly and totally[5] conditions us. I have no real fear for the future of the past when it comes to the general attitude to history, no fear that has not been present for 200 years: that is to say, I think that England could do with knowing more about her past, but that's always been so.

The academic situation of course is different. You, Mr Vice-Chancellor, have referred to the Council of the Senate. When in the course of last year I inadvertently found myself rather early for such a meeting I had recourse to the only reading available in the Council Room, which are old copies of *The Reporter*; and I discovered that precisely forty years ago there were more undergraduates studying history in this University than there are now – and the University since then has trebled in total numbers. In 1928 one in every four undergraduates read history. Nowadays the figure is approximately one in twelve. I think one in twelve is still

[4] This is the sort of example that jumps to mind in the middle of a lecture. But its surface triviality should not hide the reality of the point made. Both the English and their critics too often mistake a liking for ceremonial and pomp for a genuine awareness of the past. In fact, there is no country in which memories are notoriously shorter; nowhere else are actions – political, social, even personal – less influenced by earlier events or decisions; nowhere else does the present regard itself as less committed by what happened in history.

[5] Totally? Well, well.

too many, but one in four is quite appalling. The responsibility is too much. The consequences are not encouraging. I can see no virtue in preserving such a monopoly on the side of the humane studies as that figure suggests, and I see therefore no immediate reason to regret, as some of us are inclined to regret, the fact that the number of history students is in decline, and may well continue to decline. None of this really matters. What matters is the history which in all this process we convey. And you know, if you are thinking about the dangers to academic history, and the decline of numbers and the contraction of the subject, there is one point which you should be aware of and which you should remember. There may be fewer people reading the History Tripos. There may possibly be fewer historians ultimately practising in this University. But I seem to see an enormous colonizing activity which is already very successful. Wherever you look at subjects which had no historical dimension in their thinking, they are busily grasping it, demanding it, anxious to become historians themselves. If I today do not attack the social sciences, it is not only because I have done it before, and it is a tiresome and stupid attitude, but it is because in fact the social sciences have become converted. You don't want to listen to the established figures. You talk to the young men who are working on the ground, as they say (in the social sciences it is very much on the ground, nose to the ground); they are all trying to learn about history and the historical method, and to apply it. We have already got our conquests, we need not make them any further; we have conquered so much that we have introduced a historical dimension into almost every subject you can think of – even into the sciences where those who increasingly find that the experimental subjects of physical studies are exhausted are turning to the history of science, not only because it is an interesting occupation which fills in the long winter evenings but also because it helps them in understanding the task on which they themselves are engaged. The academic world has never been so historical, I think, in all the past.

It therefore becomes increasingly vital to know what we ourselves as historians are doing and should be doing, and what by our historical activities we produce amongst ourselves and others. What attitude, what concepts, what conclusions, what state of mind? Now again, of course, there is nothing very new about this. We have discussed this at length. But it seems to me that the remedies and problems have been rather ill-stated. If I am not mistaken, the charges levelled at historians at the present time, the grounds on which their activities are attacked as socially insufficiently useful, are in the main two. Historians, it is said, are too concerned with the parish pump. They are too concerned with their own domestic local causes. They are at best too much concerned with their own country and nation. And on the other hand they are too much occupied with matters political, many of them perhaps with details of legal and constitutional cases and things of that kind. All this has often been said, and there is still a lot of truth in it. They are, it is said, not giving a lead. They dissect, they analyse, they briefly describe, but they do not offer an answer to the great questions which move men. What will the future be? What help can the past offer to the future? And that is what they must do, we are told. And they can only do it by ridding themselves of the parochial straitjacket, by remembering the world, the great world, and by investing in new ways of looking at history, of which the most important is a grasp of society, because society asks for answers, society looks for help, society looks for guidance; and we must study society, tell it what it is, and therefore give it its hope for the future, its prospects, perhaps its stiffening of backbone.

Now I don't quarrel with these demands in many ways. I certainly do not wish to say that social history is not a remarkably important field of study. It is. I do not myself want to see all historians confining themselves to their own country or their own parish. On the contrary. But I do not think that these points are important. I do not think these points answer. I do not think that here lies the problem or the solution. For one thing, of course, we must get quite clear whether we can do anything at all. Do we really read this problem aright? Is the historian a teacher to his society, to his time? Thinking about this I ran into a quotation from Sir Richard Morison. Sir Richard Morison was one of Henry VIII's propagandists. That doesn't necessarily make him a liar. And on one occasion he wrote in one of his propaganda pamphlets – the one called *A Remedy for Sedition*, perhaps a remedy we now require – 'Education, evil education', he says, 'is a great cause of these [that is, sedition] and other mischiefs that grow in a commonwealth.' Should we really be practising education? Are we not overestimating it as a power for good, or possibly underestimating it as a power for evil? Ought we not sometimes to stand away from the whole question of education? But we all practise education; all of us here, at whatever stage of the process we are, are involved in it. It is a livelihood, it's an enterprise, but it may be a folly, it may be the 'cause of these and other mischiefs that grow in a commonwealth', and I think it very often is. Historians' educational activities have very often been precisely that. When they have been at their most instructive, most determined to instruct, they have very often been at their most disastrous.

There are obvious examples one cites on these points, like the famous case of the nineteenth-century German historians – all, we gather, men who carried a pen in one hand and a rather rusty sword in the other. And many of them did, though not all by any means. I would like to choose a very different example, one of the great revered of our own tradition. I don't think there has been a historian at work in this country who has had a worse, more disastrous effect upon what I may call the national self-consciousness than that very good man Richard Tawney.[6] With great regret I am coming to think increasingly that there is not a single work which Tawney wrote which can be trusted. I think that in all his work he was so dominated by his preconceptions, unconsciously (well, partly unconsciously), that everything he wrote was written to a propaganda purpose. And the result has been very drastic. People won't believe this, but when the historian comes to write – if an historian still comes to write – an intellectual history of the early twentieth century, Tawney will be one of the figures he will really have to concern himself with. Not Toynbee, whose influence is neither here nor there (not in this country at any rate). Not Maitland, who carried very little influence in the public mind, even indirectly. But Tawney, who wrote for a purpose – wrote beautifully, and wrote history which was in great parts – I am looking for a polite word – in great parts mistaken. And it was mistaken because he meant it to be so, though he didn't know this. He was proving a point. But

[6] This, I know, is an unpalatable remark which will give offence. It rests, however, on sad experience. *Religion and the Rise of Capitalism*, for instance, demonstrates Tawney's fatal propensity to fit a selection from a great mass of material into a predetermined framework. The picture of puritan or protestant thinking on social problems is so one-sided and so readily destroyed by admitting overlooked evidence to the analysis that the effect which the book has had must give one pause. In a forthcoming book, Dr E. Kerridge will also uncover Tawney's other serious deficiency, his failure to understand the technical problems of highly technical evidence, which led him totally to distort reality in his other influential book, *The Agrarian Problem of the Sixteenth Century*. [E. Kerridge, *Agrarian Problems in the Sixteenth Century and After* (London, 1969).] Because Tawney, a great man, had a real concern about his own world, he wrote very effective history, but it was also history in blinkers, confirming present-based prejudices and attitudes from an investigation of the past which came up with the answers required by the faith that inspired the search. But behind this possibly commonplace trouble lay the remediable failure to consider all the evidence and to understand the manner in which it came into existence.

the whole collapse of self-confidence which we have encountered in this present generation – while it owes a great deal, I know, to 'forces' and 'factors' (both these words are in quotes) outside any man's competence, owes an immense amount to the influence of this one man and his school, percolating through the public press into the minds of the leaders of opinion, the intellectual leaders of society. Not only the academics, but also the men who write, and the men who read.

Tawney's effect may or may not be regarded as good for England and the world – I don't know. One has one's different views on this, of course. The point I'm making is that a man like Tawney, who apparently wrote history but was determined to instruct, produced consequences which were quite incommensurate to the cause, and which were derived from the fact that his history was not good, not sound, not right, not true. And if we are going to do this kind of thing, if we believe despite all our apprehensions that education may be necessary and useful, if we believe despite all our apprehensions that the historian must contribute to the public mind, let us for Heaven's sake make sure that we get right both the disease which we are trying to cure and the remedy which we try to provide.

Now what is the disease? To suppose that those who attack historians for being too parochial and too much concerned with the details of political history and such-like are right is to suppose that what is wrong with the world at present is an excessive concentration upon one's own country and nation and an excessive concentration on the particular, an absence of general theories, an inability and unwillingness to read large, to look large, to think large. I don't believe this is true. Again I was thinking about these points when I encountered another very useful thing: a certain advertisement in *The Times* which instructed over some signatures – you are familiar with it – a very large number of people in their present duty in assisting the country in its troubles.[7] I looked – hopefully, and anxiously – for what a historian can do to back Britain; and the answer appears to be, in the opinion of the eminent successful institutions that signed this manifesto, nothing – not a thing. Well, I think he can do something. I would suggest to you what the historian can do is to create a state of mind in which an advertisement of this kind is impossible, which puts an end to this kind of rubbishy thinking, this nonsensical piece of propaganda. And not only this; this is only a small example. What is wrong with the world today? Not that people lack prophets; they fall for every prophet there is. Has there ever been an age in the history of the world in which faith was more apparent and less reasonable? Has there ever been an age in the history of the world in which the outpourings of Professor Marshall McLuhan could be taken seriously by very large numbers of intellectuals, people trained academically, because they believe that in some way or other technological change has eliminated the mind, eliminated the voice, eliminated the eyes and reduced everything to some kind of mercury vapour? This is not a day of sceptics, this is not a day of unbelievers. We are living in one of the ages of faith, and that the faith is not attached to institutionalized religion does not disprove the point that I have just made. On the contrary: it renders the faiths more varied, more easy. They come in all shapes and sizes, some more respectable, some less. There are Freudians and there are Marxists, and these are respectable because they have been here a long time. And there are believers in psychedelics, anti-psychedelics, universities and anti-universities. Every-

---

[7] The reference was to the full-page advertisement placed in *The Times* of 7 February 1968 by the 'How to Help Britain and Yourself Campaign'. This made a number of 'uncranky suggestions' for action to a range of people from 'mums' through millionaires to everyone. I do not doubt that this curious piece was meant sincerely or that people might well on occasion follow its advice, but this does not derogate from the fact that it displayed a total confusion about real issues and a mindless appeal to the irrational.

thing is a matter of faith, nothing is a matter of reason. People look for prophets. It is no wonder that this appeal found the support of Professor Arnold Toynbee. The world is littered with prophets and gurus. The world is desperately seeking for answers of that kind.

Now we as historians can most certainly, if we want to, cash in on that. We can say, 'Very well then, we will be your prophets, we will supply your need, we will fill your faith-hungry souls with the faith that may not move mountains but will certainly move money from one pocket into another.' But are we wise to do so? We can gain a temporary success. We can destroy the life of the mind. We can assist in that anti-reason, that attack on the reason, which, it seems to me, is the most marked feature of the age in which we live. Now of course we should not do that. Even rhetorical questions should not be quite so obvious in their answer as the one which I have just put to you. Of course we should not do it. We are here as defenders of reason and thought, of the proper assessment and proper study of evidence, and this is what we are here to teach the world. Therefore, if I am right in thinking that what this age needs is an anti-faith, is the reality of thought, then the historian's task becomes a different one. It is not a question of finding an answer to the future, of planning the future, of settling the future for the world. All he can do is tell them about the past in such a way that they can think better about past, present and future. And how is he to do that?

The other thing which I suggested to you dominates public discussion on this point is that we suffer from an excess of patriotism or parochialism; but again I don't see this – not in this country at least – where are the patriots? The last generation of people who unthinkingly went to war died in the last war, or, if they survived, lost their unthinking attachment to it. We are all today the product – if we are the product of anything at all – of the 1930s and 40s, and that was not a good time to be born and bred in, as we all know; the age bears the consequences, the scars, the terrible mental scars, which those two decades left. Scars heal up to a point, and we must allow them to heal and try to rise above such things, but we are no longer patriots, we are no longer parochial. We are more ready to believe in China and Peru than in Runcorn and Southampton. And if our particular studies seem parochial, if our historical studies seem to concern themselves with the particular and the detail, this is not because people do not go out and remember the world, but because they just want to learn to do this particular historical job on a piece of parochial study. Many others do not – and work on other things. But there is no parish-pump mind left in this country that I can see. On the contrary, turn your back on your own country is getting to be practically the order of the day – or at least do not turn your back on it, because then you'll have to back it, but insist on seeing nothing but ill in it.

Let us remember Richard Morison once again. He was praising the splendour of England, the wealthiest of nations, where everything was so plentiful and so easily got that it was the idlest country that he knew, and he knew quite a few. People worked for three days a week because they didn't have to work any longer, unlike the unfortunate French and Italians, and they ate so well: 'I will not compare our keeping of houses with theirs, where frogs be a dainty dish, snails a morsel for a lady, mushrooms stand for the second course' – mushrooms stand for the second course. These are all things we now regard as specialities, as delicacies. So far have we sunk. We think that frogs are a dainty dish, and snails a morsel for a lady, and most of us eat mushrooms for the last course, now and again. Richard Morison's and the sixteenth century's overelaborated patriotism, to put it mildly, is something which we need not copy. But why should we fall right over into the other extreme? There is still a great deal to be said for living in this country, and the historian's task consists among other things, if I may so put it, in a crude rekindling of a certain respect for a country whose past justifies that respect.[8]

But the main task is of course different, the main task is the one I spoke of before, the creation of a right mind, and a right reason, and in this the historian, like every other intellectual worthy of the name, is concerned with one thing only: to discover the truth as best he can, to convey that truth as truthfully as he can, in order both to make the truth known and to enable man, by learning and knowing the truth, to distinguish the right from the wrong reason. That is the simple historian's task, as it is every other academic teacher's task; and I can therefore see no virtue in the claim that we must devise the future. We cannot. None of us sitting here are any better qualified than any man alive to tell what the future may be, and only, I think, an overweening self-confidence enables us to suggest that we know what the future should be. We can hope, we can pray, we can act, but we cannot reason, we cannot teach, we cannot discover. We can only make sure that those who enter that future have a mind of the right quality, the capacity to think clearly, precisely and within the limits, the limitations, of the human reason. We must not preach to men a hope which no one can fulfil. Leave that to the prophets, leave that to the faiths. We must confine ourselves to the task which we can fulfil, to bring to men the release of thought. And if we historians should want to do that, I am afraid we have to be

---

[8] No one wants to re-create a crude chauvinism or an unthinking conservatism. My quarrel is with the other side of that same coin, equally crude and unthinking, which can suppose that only Britain is beset by certain universal troubles like egotism, snobbery, prudery or class-consciousness, that somewhere else everything is better, and that the nation's achievements in the past are to be comprehensively condemned. It remains true – a fact of history and a fact of experience – that this country is still in many ways the most civilized to live in, that in its history it has accomplished many admirable and humanly profitable things, and that its record of sensible actions need cause no shame to anyone.

very old fashioned. We have to concern ourselves, not only with the past, but also with the past's attitude to the past, with the things that are traditional in our not ill-tried profession. We shall have to continue to think in terms of what is the evidence, what does it tell? What can it be made to yield? What does reason make of the evidence? We cannot seek refuge in the generalities which others provide. We cannot accept our answers before we have looked at our questions. We cannot plan and plot the thing we would like; we have to stick by the thing that we find that *is*. And in this context, to come back to what, I think (if I remember rightly), was my starting-point, in this context the well-tried traditional subject of English Constitutional History continues to play its eminent part.

I want to make quite plain what I think English constitutional history is and means. I don't have a programme for it; I do not presume to impose a notion of what should be on anybody except myself; but I would like to explain to you what I believe the task of this particular compartment of historical studies really is. Like all these categories, it has its own history. For a long time the study of English government and other forms of government was very largely a matter of discovering law and legal practices. Not so long ago we passed a very intensive phase of what has come to be known as administrative history. Everybody wanted to know exactly how a particular system worked, or where each particular officer stood, and what they were doing; and this indeed is still a very necessary and active part of the study. But all of it, and other forms, seem to me to be subject to one very general and particular purpose. The purpose of constitutional history is to study government, the manner in which men, having formed themselves into societies, then arrange for the orderly existence, through time, and in space, of those societies. It is therefore, like every other form of history, a form of social history, a form of the history of society. But it takes particular note of the question of

government. It is concerned with what is done to make that
society into a properly structured, continuously living body,
so that what goes wrong can be put right, so that the
political action of which that society is capable can be
efficiently and effectively conducted. Machinery, yes. But
also thought, the doctrine, the teaching, the conventional
notions. What does the society think its government is, how
does it treat it, what does it do to amend it? What forms of
change are possible, what reforms, and so on and so forth. It
is neither purely constitutional history of the old kind – it is
not a case of precedents and cases – nor is it administrative
history of the old kind – it is not a case of analysing quite
simply (I'm sorry, very unsimply, very complicatedly) what
actually happens when government is in action, or what
machinery there is which the government has at its disposal.
It is not a case of political theory, what is being taught about
the nature of politics and the nature of government. It is all
those things. It treats a living social organism in one particular activity – the activity of governing itself.[9]

This, I think, will sound very vague and rather vapoury,
but it is not when it comes to the point. If you take any
given problem in the government of any given country you
have to treat it, it seems to me, from this multiplicity of
points of view. You have to see it both as a machine and as a

---

[9] In all this stress on society as the subject of historical study, I quite
forgot to mention the weight to be given to individuals, to the
activities of identifiable men and women, which it is one of the tasks
of sound history constantly to remember. Constitutional history,
properly conceived, enables the historian to attend also to this task,
for its approach and concern make the actions and reactions of people
better discernible than they are in such ways of study as economic or
social history, whether of the old or the new kind. The relations
between society and the individual are one of the major problems of
all government, and though anthropologically or sociologically
directed studies can sometimes help to analyse them, they are still
best tackled by a specific investigation from the records of political
action.

thought, and as a sequence of legalizations, and all those things, but in the main you have to see it, overall you have to see it, as the product of social life, the life of society expressing itself in this way; and the great virtue of this form of historical study is purely technical. It happens to be the activity of society which is always going to be most fully recorded and most clearly apprehensible. There are many things we do as social and individual beings and many of them record themselves; but none so systematically, none so continuously, none so far back into the past in such plenitude as the activities of government – for very obvious reasons: the recording is done by government; the recording will always be done by those who rule, in the various senses that that word implies, because they require a record; they require to know what has been and what is done, and they will therefore continue to record. Therefore, from the point of view both of the continuous work of historical research and from the point of view of teaching history, and from the point of view of conveying to the world and to the future a sense of the past and an understanding of the past, the study of government maintains, to my mind, its primacy. It can be most fully explicated, it can be most thoroughly described, it can be most clearly understood, it leaves fewer absolutely open questions, it can instruct in the use of reason better than anything else.

But, once that reason is so instructed, let it go on. Once that reason has learned its business, let it spread itself, let it go forth into other studies of all kinds, let it even go and run Marks & Spencers, let it go and produce newspapers, let it go and be active in the world. I am not preaching a single contraction to the activity of constitutional history. The world is fortunately, very fortunately, a great deal larger than that; and if ever we think in our studies and in our lecture rooms that what we do here is what matters most, I think we should say this in public; but we should in private know very differently. We should indeed be very assertive about ourselves, because no one else will be. The world will only take note of those who believe in themselves. The world will only be considerate to those who tread on its toes. But amongst ourselves, in our privacy, in our cell, we should know better than that, and if we don't we'll do bad work. If we are humble outwardly and proud inwardly I think we ought to be turned inside out like a good glove, and we shall be better for the world that way. But let us persuade ourselves, let us persuade those that matter, future generations, present generations, rulers and ruled, the men with the money, the men with the patronage, the men with the gifts, let us persuade them that what we have to contribute to their future work is that understanding of right reason and true faith, faith based on knowledge, faith based on really hard thinking, which historical study is so magnificently constructed to supply. I am not for one moment asking you to abandon your faiths; only the wrong faiths. Learn about the right ones. I am not trying to preach the nothing. Scepticism is what I call for, but scepticism is not nihilism, scepticism is equal to a positive assessment of the truth. Scepticism is not, believe me, the same thing as seeing everything relative. We can be positive about all our knowledge and all our discoveries and all our understanding of the past. We don't have to tell the world: 'Well, it all depends, it's just what this or that historian has made of it.' That isn't true. We can tell them quite positively, very often: we know because we have thought, we know because we have worked, we know because we have learned, and we are willing to tell you so. We do not know everything, and we never shall. We do not know with absolute certainty everything that we now take for knowledge. We may change our minds, yes. But we have minds – minds to change as well as minds to keep. Let us be sceptical. Let us be neither devout nor unthinking. [10]

[10] I have tried to make the case for the historian's activity in discovering a truth independent of himself in *The Practice of History* (1967), pp. 51 ff.

And if we do that, then I think we shall give the future a past which is worth having. Then that past will become memorable and influential and important, and will be the foundation of things that matter, because out of it will grow a positive, active, burgeoning reason which will do much to destroy the unreasons and the horrors of the mind which infest the world. No one can do anything about the horrors of the deed. No one here. We cannot end wars. Why should we? Why should we think we could? We cannot end folly, we cannot end mistakes and all the errors the flesh is subject to. But we can do our best to produce an end to the false mind, to the prophetic mini-mind which at the moment dominates so much of this world. We can teach the world that to ask for the answers before we have done the work of finding them is bad. We can teach the world that to flood everything with specifics is bad; that remedies depend upon an understanding, and not upon a hope. These are the things which we as historians can teach.

In doing this we shall, I think, be much attacked. We shall be told – we are being told – that all we want to do is confine ourselves to the simple, academic, homely atmosphere in which it is so pleasant to live. Those who speak in these terms seem to know very little about the academic atmosphere. I do not deny that it is a very pleasant atmosphere to live in, but it is neither peaceful nor mollifying. It is pungent. It smells. It smells of sulphur and cordite. It's a battle line. The hospitals are full of the casualties. We shall be told that we abandon and resign the task of helping the world over its stile to others less well qualified, to others less well able to do it perhaps, or at any rate to others. Well, I suggest we should. One of the things we should abandon is the notion that we can give the world its future pattern to live by. It is our task to tell the social scientists (who will after all insist on coming in on this discourse) – to tell the social scientists to shut up. To keep their remedies to their books and not to try on the *corpus vile* of unfortunate mankind the solutions which they propound. And why? Not because they themselves are foolish or vicious or anything like that, but because we know as historians that they are bound to be wrong. (I have yet to prove this point.) Time and again remedies are proposed by those who think that they have analysed the historical and present situation, and therefore forecast the future. Each time the remedies proposed apply to the past situation – never to the present. They are always out of date. Look at the history of economic advice given to governments over the last hundred years. It was always advice eminently suited to the experience of the previous generation, and it was bound to be so, because they based themselves on experience; they wanted to be empirical; they thought they were doing the right thing. You historians, they will say, have told us that we must study the past, we must understand the past, and that is what we are doing. We are learning from fact, we are not imposing our schemes. Quite right. They think they are not. But they are learning from the past to do something for the present and future. The historian should tell them that this cannot be done, that this is not the way to do it; that the remedies for 1930 are not the remedies for 1960 – are bound to be different; and that studying the past teaches nothing about the present and the future in that 'learn it, apply it' method. It is for that reason that they are bound to be wrong; for that reason that we as historians can teach them.

We are confronted by prophets, we are confronted by social remediers and organizers, and they are both dangerous men; men who apply ready-made answers to complex human situations. If the world is to survive, if the intellect, which matters, is to survive, historians have a task of immense construction and not at all of destruction. I remember an occasion some years ago – one of those not uncommon occasions, I fear – on which I spoke too passionately on some point or other, when a friend in kindly rebuke quoted at me that most touching, perhaps most marvellous, of all sen-

tences of defiance: 'Victrix causa deis placuit, sed victa
Catoni.' I need not in this company translate. It is a sentence
which I have found, and continue to find, immensely consoling. They are indeed victorious gods and defeated men, but
the gods against whom I have today pleaded for your aid,
against whom I have tried to enlist you in a battle line, are
false gods, and bound to die. But since they are gods, they
will, I fear, outlive those of us present here to a man, and a
woman. We shall none of us see them die. But we must
work towards it nonetheless, for die they will. To have
stood, however briefly, however feebly, however unavail-
ingly, for the cause of reason and the cause of truth at some
time in one's life will on that day of their death occasion
some just and very overweening pride in whatever Elysian
corner of the universe our human consciousness may then
survive.

The History of England:
Inaugural Lecture as
Regius Professor of Modern History
in the University of Cambridge,
1984

In 1724, the elector of Hanover, engaged as king of England in founding a monarchic dynasty, endowed a chair of modern history at the University of Cambridge. (Also at Oxford, of course, but that is not this day a matter of major concern.) In 1808, one Samuel Meyer Ehrenberg, engaged (though he did not know it) in founding a modest scholarly dynasty, took over an ailing school at Wolfenbüttel, a few miles from Hanover though then in the neighbouring duchy of Brunswick. In 1983, a descendant of the former bestowed her ancestor's foundation upon a descendant of the latter, thus keeping things within the old territorial relations. Indeed, the connexion was symbolized even more clearly. The elector of Hanover and the duke of Brunswick, both being Guelphs, were in a manner of speaking cousins; and in 1983 the holders of both those Regius chairs at Oxford and Cambridge are cousins too. There is a certain satisfactory rotundity about these essentially improbable events.

When I look back upon the history of the chair which now I have the great honour to occupy, I find myself even more impressed than usual by the mysterious ways of providence, or rather, perhaps, by the unpredictability of human purposes manifestly not controlled by providence. For about a century and a half the existence of Regius professors of modern history in this university could easily have escaped notice, though a few of them gave lectures. The chair was in fact precisely 151 years old when at last the academic claims of history found recognition here, by the inappropriate but normal device of turning it into a tripos of its own. The achievement belonged to the first truly notable Regius professor, Sir John Seeley, who, by the way, died in office one year younger in age than is the present occupant upon taking up his duties. Seeley had succeeded to Charles Kingsley, the last of the absurdities, and his inaugural lecture provided the occasion for the finest double anti-compliment ever uttered: a story so familiar that I will not repeat it here. I have good reason to feel that this time, too, an inaugural lecture will induce regrets for the departure of my predecessor, but on this occasion there will be no implication adverse to the retired tenant. To succeed to Owen Chadwick is both an honour and a burden. How can one possibly expect to emulate one who rather gave distinction to the chair than derived distinction from it? He will, I think, prove to have been the last honestly qualified Regius professor of modern history, for the modern history of King George's devising is all history since the fall of Rome. And here we had a man who took all modern history as his province, giving it lustre wherever he touched it. *The Times* newspaper has already inadvertently extended his tenure into mine, and quite right too. While he lives, Owen will remain *the* Regius professor: I and my successors will always acknowledge his primacy.

Since 1875, history and its professor, soon joined by other persons of the same standing though never by a professor of English history until Sir John Plumb and I wrote the mark of chauvinism into our temporary titles, have increasingly flourished in this university. Nor was this only – though until the English tripos rose to prominence this was often the case – because history provided a refuge for those undergraduates who had to pretend to read something if they were to be admitted at all. History and its professors did indeed offer this service to a university anxious to attract fee-paying members – a service of which, to judge by some of the things I have heard said, an echo is still to be found in the M.Phil. in international studies spawned by the History Faculty. However, the faculty and the university increasingly promoted the real thing too. The greatest of our historians, alas, was never Regius professor or indeed a member of the History Faculty: F. W. Maitland always disguised himself, not too successfully, as a lawyer. But the descent from Seeley testifies to the effect that a laying-on of hands will have, even though now and again (and I am told that this happens also in the Church) the hands alit upon somewhat surprising heads. Lord Acton, J. B. Bury, G. M. Trevelyan, G. N. Clark, J. R. M. Butler, David Knowles, Herbert Butterfield, Owen Chadwick: four knights, three heads of Houses, two OMs, one lord leaping – and one exclaustrated Benedictine. To write G. R. Elton after that does strike a discordant note of bathos. Ah well: a chair that survived such an inaugural address as Acton's, prescribing a regime which he had never succeeded in carrying out himself, should have no difficulty in surviving mine: some sort of consolation for the future.

What purpose did King George have in mind when in pudding-time he came over to introduce the University of Cambridge to the existence of a history that was neither Graeco-Roman nor, as they called it, ethnic? (There is a term of confusion for you: the present propagandists for ethnic history should know that they are really advocating a study of the begats of the Old Testament.) Though Cambridge was unaware, England knew about it all right – an England which had produced William Camden, John Selden, Henry Spelman, Humphrey Wanley, Thomas Madox – and only the universities needed to be apprised of the fact. The King made his purpose plain. It had come to his notice that the English universities neglected precisely those studies which were needed to train servants of the state, particularly diplomats, who all needed to know modern history and foreign languages, the teaching of the latter being committed to lecturers which the professors were to pay out of their £40 stipends. (No such lecturers, not surprisingly, seem ever to have been appointed.) People, said the royal critic, wanting to acquire those useful skills were forced to rely on foreign tutors, a sad state of affairs. He intended his foundation to remedy these defects and thereby give academic institutions immersed in the study of the ancients a chance to contribute to current concerns. In accepting his gift, Cambridge looked forward to the time when 'a familiarity with the living tongues should be super-added to the dead ones ... and when the appearance of an English gentleman in the courts of Europe with a governor of his own nation would not be so rare and uncommon as it theretofore had been'. (For the early history of the Regius chair I refer myself to Maitland's introduction to a collection entitled *Essays on the Teaching of History*, published by the University Press in 1901. The essays show how little has changed in either ambitions or achievements in eighty years.)

In reality, the King wanted more than native tutors for young noblemen doing the Grand Tour. He was not the last man to compare the English universities with those of his own country, to the detriment of Oxford and Cambridge. At home he was used to universities that concentrated on training the people the state relied on for the staffing of its services – theologians to run the state-dominated territorial churches, and jurists to run the secular administrations. In England he found institutions that consistently neglected the needs of government, producing clergy who no longer served the state and lightly polished gentlemen who with luck could read Horace on sight. So he set up professors of modern history and hoped for lecturers in languages. In return – what else do we expect? – he received words of praise which spoke well of those lecturers that were never set to the task and which altogether neglected to mention the professors of modern history. Still, it is quite a thought that this chair was founded for much the same reasons as those that today cause governments and social reformers to intrude upon our academic concerns.

As academic developments go, the 150 years that elapsed before King George I's real purpose was picked up and given some reality are not a terribly long time. Seeley also wished to use history to train governors of the realm, and from his tenure onwards Cambridge came increasingly to view the teaching of history in that light. Gradually history graduates overtook classicists as the mainstay of the civil service, and some of them joined a knowledge of French or even German to the wisdom they had gained from reading Stubbs. Until a generation ago one quite regularly encountered the opinion that the only respectable modern history to read – the only one that stretched the mind – was medieval; we have in our own day heard impassioned claims for the exclusive virtue of studies that terminate before the Reformation. I do not mean to decry medieval history – far from it. In particular I do not wish to give praise to really modern history, at a time when the history of the last hundred years in turn threatens to lay claim to being the only respectable form of modern history. I am anxious to remember that the chair I now hold pertains to all history since the fifth century, a fact which imposes a vast and unaccustomed tolerance upon its occupant. What has at times troubled me are the effects of overpraising the middle ages; such attitudes have before this prevented other bits of history from acquiring the right foundations of learning because medievalists have degraded them to an inbuilt inferiority.

However, such things, I hope, are in the past, as unhappily also is the notion that the study of modern history should be associated with the learning of foreign languages. There are still universities in this country which demand a knowledge of French or German and so forth from any undergraduates who wish to study history, but Cambridge no longer belongs to that oldfangled group. When, in order to accommodate our scientists, we by stages dismantled language qualifications for matriculation we surrendered a safeguard of academic quality in the University at large. Moreover, our History Faculty, unlike sister departments elsewhere, is not allowed to impose its own linguistic conditions because we must be prepared to let chemists or sociologists read one part of our tripos who are free to come to the study of their other specialism without such compulsion. Pressed for money, the Seeley Historical Library has pretty well ceased to buy books in languages other than English, though admittedly some of the recent work in social history, especially but not only from the United States, in effect demands a knowledge of a difficult variant of the mother tongue. Put a book written in French or German on the shelves, and it will retain its pristine beauty – an untouchable ice princess among the much handled, much defaced crowd of more promiscuous sisters. When recently I included two essays in German in a volume of collected papers – on the grounds that they had been written and published in that language – one reviewer blamed me for not translating them first.

So one of George I's purposes has been ignored by the historians of Cambridge, nor is the existence of a tripos of modern and medieval languages much excuse for that lapse. The other purpose, it seems to me, is in danger of going the same way. True, for a hundred years or so we have been using the study of history for the training of state servants, for the preparation of properly educated minds capable of judging a situation, of assessing human beings, of fitting their actions into traditions so that if change was needed it would at least have a reasonable chance of actually working. We have also kept the study of history alive and flourishing by something that neither George I nor any public figure of his time thought significant – by the practice of fruitful historical research and the training of our successors. This, however, is a theme that I do not propose to discuss today. Nor do I wish to consider the studies which we are increasingly urged to substitute for history in our preparation of public servants and their like. If the time ever comes that we shall be governed by graduates in the social sciences or computer studies or perhaps linguistics, there will be a darkness at noon which will call for the services of the historian to restore the light of day. Historians take long views: we can wait for our return to the favour which for a century landed us with undergraduates of whom many had only a marginal interest in what we were talking about. In any case, for the present the hostile voices, however loud, come from quite a small minority, though it includes men of influence. I see some signs of premature panic among colleagues which I cannot regard as appropriate to the *iucunda gravitas* of our profession. Those hostile voices sound strongest in the lower reaches of our schools, and if this means that more people will escape having all interest in history drummed out of them before they are old enough to like looking at the past, so much the better.

What I want to consider today is one phenomenon which seems to me to lie behind the decline of history as a study for the servants of the state and which has received surprisingly little attention. The modern history we have used in the past to educate our students always included a variety of ages, countries and nations, but it gathered around a central theme, the history of England. In some places it still does, mainly because they do not have experts in Mexico or Malawi to vary the diet drastically. But here it does not, nor does it flourish anywhere any longer with that coherent confidence in an ordered story which made the undergraduate study of history satisfying and the virtues of historical studies immediately apparent, however far removed it might be from the real professional investigation of any part of it. In the last thirty years or so it has, I think, become accepted wisdom that there is a lot of history outside England, a point not unknown to all of us but by some not thought altogether decisive in the construction of courses for study that had to be completed within three years. So by stages all kinds of very interesting topics have been introduced into the tripos for the double purpose of giving a wider experience to undergraduates and a voice to persuasive practitioners of other histories. Nothing, I agree, is wrong with this in principle, but the consequences have been unexpected – not unexpected by all of us – and to some extent disastrous.

Our historical tripos now lacks all cohesion and with it any real understanding of what it is trying to do; the only thing for which it is excellent is the training of that small minority of students who go on to research. In part II, our undergraduates now study a few very very short periods, and if they also offer a dissertation they specialize (allowing for the different length of their studies) quite as much as do research students, whose excessive concentrations on one topic used to be deplored by progressive reformers. Nor does part I offer a real chance to study history in perspective: specialization affects it too. No one reading our subject in this university needs to involve himself in more than about fifty years of English and perhaps a hundred years of European history. Moreover, the options on offer have multiplied so recklessly that one comes to doubt whether any two undergraduates pursue the same course. All very free and generous, and I do not in the least doubt the fascination of many of those options: though I do think it unwise to teach quite so many bits of history in which not enough people have yet worked to provide a solid body of properly criticized sources and writings. This lack tends to reduce the mind-training capacity of historical study. Worse, however, is the fact that in the process one of the chief virtues of that study has vanished as the student is never made to watch developments over a real stretch of time and is not rendered capable of measuring different experiences against each other. We cannot be doing right when we send people into the world who have graduated in history and have never been made to feel the length of it. The current list of part II dissertations leans overwhelmingly towards the last century and a half, with a high proportion of them looking at the 1930s and 1960s. For them the past reaches at best to the day before yesterday, and social studies have crept in by the backdoor. But I do not think that those for whom the past extends from 1066 to perhaps 1350 are any better off.

No one, of course, can study all history; a considerable degree of specialization is bound to prevail. So long as there is one strong element of real continuity in the course, specialization elsewhere does good. In an English university, peopled by undergraduates somewhat averse to reading foreign languages, that element of continuity would naturally be the history of England. But just as that theme became most urgently needed it lost all self-confidence and joined the rush down the specialist slope – fragmenting into ever smaller pieces, some scintillating like diamonds but others as dull as honest sand. It would seem to be widely held that this is a good thing. A course built around a long stretch of English history is likely to get called chauvinist or ethnocentric, or whatever the latest vogue word of condemnation may be: even perhaps elitist, and you can't say worse that that. It goes against the liberal grain to give the next generation a large dollop of the history of their own country; it goes against the mentality created by genuine research to give the next generation anything not worked down to the roots. Of course, there are other countries and other themes worth getting to know, but why should this mean that English students of history must really be prevented from studying this history of their own nation? I have an advantage here: I cannot be accused of mindless patriotism acquired by the accident of birth. Perhaps one who came to England and English history from outside may be allowed to break a lance for both of them.

Let us therefore now look at the kinds of argument which I have seen or heard advanced against giving English history a dominant role in English historical studies. The chief of them seems to have impressed a lot of people. It maintains that whereas at one time it was possible to tell a tale of coherent development, a tale which made sense, this cannot now be done. It is indeed the case that until, perhaps, the end of the second world war the history of England could with some conviction be construed around a dominant theme. Three such themes stood out any one of which used to serve very well. One was the history of political freedom – the story of constitutional development which tracked the roots of Mr Gladstone's House of Commons to the Anglo-Saxon Witenagemot, or at least to Magna Carta. A second was the growth of empire – the spread of the English over the world. The third, less amenable to such progressive treatment but still capable of accommodating itself to it, looked at England as the mother of industry and wrote the story around the development of trade and manufacture. All three held to a strong theme; all three underwrote notions of progress; all three ended on a high note and could thus serve the cause of self-esteem and self-satisfaction.

In addition, all three had an inestimable advantage which is too rarely recognized. They all offered a lovely stamping ground to both the admirer and the detractor. This is obviously true of the former, the bard of demi-paradises: by the time you had reached Victoria's empire, governed by an ideal constitutional monarchy through a Parliament which embodied all political wisdom, and fuelled by the ever-expanding wealth produced by science and industry, you hardly needed to explain the central significance of your story – the central significance, that is, which it held for all mankind. In England, at least, the fact that English history most convincingly demonstrated how man should order his existence on earth required no more than an apparently modest rehearsal of what had happened there in the course of a thousand years. But lo and behold: exactly the same story would serve to demonstrate the opposite with equal coherence and conviction. All you had to do was turn the medal over. What I may call the Froude complex – the belief that the blessings of providence have fallen exclusively upon this island – has always been matched by the *New Statesman* complex, the assurance that all things human are absolutely at their worst in this country. Those who praised the unique amalgam represented by a nation united under its rulers stood opposed – indeed, stand opposed – by those who know that structures and consciousness of class are found only in England. Those who looked with starry eyes upon the civilizing mission of anti-slavery frigates and heroic (if rather juvenile) district commissioners, faced the determined enemies of colonial exploitation and racial prejudice, so different, they proclaimed, from the welcome extended by France to her overseas territories. (The hallmark of the *New Statesman* complex is the belief that all things French are wonderful.) Encomia on a tolerant and kindly society (remember the unarmed policemen?) had to confront believers in the special depravity of a people of hypocrites, uniquely devoted to what was then called the English vice, whether this meant sexual aberration or oppression of the poor. Only in England, said the one side, was political freedom fully established; only in England, replied the other, was economic freedom systematically suppressed. It was such a lovely medal of which both sides made history so easy. No matter whether you put a plus or a minus sign before your construct, in either way you testified to your belief that England and her history enjoyed the special privilege of providing an example to mankind – an example of either encouragement or warning.

This simple belief has gone, though the plus sign vanished before its counterpart of which, thanks to the continued existence of the *New Statesman*, one can still find fading traces. In consequence, if I understand the argument correctly, it follows that since English history no longer has those lessons to teach there is no reason for presenting it any

longer at proper length. What virtue can there be in studying the muddled history of a small off-shore island whose
supposed achievements have turned out illusory? This abdication from prominence gets justified on one of three
grounds, two of which strike me as unconvincing while the
third does need serious consideration. Let me dispose of the
two which deserve to be called absurd. The empire is gone,
we hear, which leaves a small bit of Europe undeserving, in
its current political and social confusion, of anybody's
serious attention: what right have we to wish to concentrate
young minds upon its history? Of course, the empire has
gone, not for the first time as it happens, and of course the
country is in trouble: but why should this terminate interest
in its history? Do not those very facts make that history more
interesting and accessible, inasmuch as the subject is in a
manner concluded and can be viewed with a hindsight
untroubled by the daily addition of new developments? And
why should the decline of English, or indeed British, weight
in the world affect the case at all? Are we to study only the
history of nations that at the moment look like being
successful? In 1984, I am not sure that that principle would
leave us with any history worth studying. Where is Bohun,
where is Bigod, where is Mortimer – all right. Perhaps even
where is Lloyd George, where is Winston Chruchill, where
is Wedgwood Benn. But how do we stand on where is
Franklin Delano Roosevelt, where is Vladimir Illyitch
Lenin?

I do not seem to have heard similarly humble consider-
ations advanced in other countries that have undergone a
decline in power and influence. So the reasons behind this
peculiar argument really boil down to the second absurd
proposition: since we have lost the sense of superiority that
used to sustain us, we can no longer ask anyone – not even
English men and women – to concern themselves at length
with the history of this country. Sackcloth and ashes, expiat-
ing for past arrogance. We have discovered that we have

nothing to teach, only to learn, and we thus must send ourselves and our children to school in the history of the United States, of China, above all of that curious extra-terrestrial place known as the Third World. In teaching, though not as yet in research in which reality has a way of shouldering fantasy aside, all things outside Europe are more glamorous than anything European, and within Europe these islands bring up a rear which is best ignored. Those of us who thought that we had succeeded in stemming the tide of Toynbeeism are beginning to realize that we crowed too soon. The extravagances of his bizarre scales of values pene-trated more deeply into academic consciousness than I for one had understood.

However, as I have said, I feel myself unusually well qualified to preach against this sort of defeatism. Coming to country and history only in my late teens, I can emphasize to you the special virtues of both without risking charges of inborn chauvinism and narrowness of mind. My experience of other countries stems not from reading about them or visiting them: I have lived in several, and while I lived there had no inkling that I might come to live here. Let me therefore say quite simply this: England is, perhaps was, different from any other country I know at first or second hand. As a society and a body politic it is unique in ways which are exceptionally instructive and, considering the nature of man and of the world he has built for himself, exceptionally consoling. I am not suffering from the Froude complex. I know very well that this is not a realm of unfailing virtue and goodness. That does not alter the fact that it managed to produce a form of existence which is freer of sin against one's neighbour than any other community has attained. I know as well as anyone that its managements, its unions, its weather and its restaurants stand a long way behind qualities easily attained elsewhere. But it excels in having come to terms with the fact that people in large numbers need both to be conscious of one another and leave one another alone. Its people have contributed disproportionately to the stock of human invention and achievement, and they have done so in ways which testify to the differences that make the English so peculiar in the eyes of the conventional Europeans. And since it is obviously desirable to understand how an organism so untypical and yet so generally successful actually worked, the history of England retains its special claim to attention.

If I am told that difference and success lie in the past – that England has now abandoned both its singularity and its power to achieve anything – I, who at times find myself leaning to that opinion too, must stress that this makes engagement with the country's history even more important. History is the study of the past; England is past; ergo, we should concentrate upon its history. Perhaps we may pick up some lessons for the present, but in an age which avidly seeks to use history for this inappropriate and usually misleading purpose we should not trouble ourselves too much about that. No matter what history we study or teach, the generality, led by traitors within the camp, will in any case think that it needs the past only in order to confirm the misguided prejudices and errors by which it orders its present. We cannot prevent this, though we can stop ourselves from pandering to it; and by sticking to history as it was we may even force people to take note of a real rather than a contrived past. However, I commend the study of English history not because it teaches lessons but because it is concerned with a most uncommon phenomenon, so peculiar and special that it can help to correct a great many one-sided views about the past and about mankind. The fact that that history, by the side of a record of folly and horror, tells much that is reassuring about the human animal, its skills and its intelligence and its occasional good sense, is a bonus but it does not constitute the main reason for studying the history of England in a long perspective. That main reason lies in the fact that it offers a singularly helpful way

for coming to terms with the past, and a singularly instructive guide to the variety of the past.

In the long perspective: it is here that the third objection,
the only one that strikes me as valid, puts in its word. This
points out that the proliferation of historical research has
made it impossible to contrive any reasonably coherent
framework in which a long stretch of English history might
be accommodated: everything we say has its exception, and
there are no great themes left. The progress of knowledge
has afflicted English history in two ways. In the first place it
has destroyed the comfortable assumptions of the older view
which was specifically useful for King George's purpose –
the view that one should structure English history around
the growth of constitutional freedoms and especially the
history of Parliament. Secondly, it looks as though there is
now so much particular history about – such various and
often contested details to take into account – that it is futile
even to attempt to pull our understanding into a story which
can cover more than a few decades – a century at most, and
even that is difficult.

Having spent most of my career in denouncing and
demolishing received wisdom, I am very conscious of the
fact that a long-lived and comprehensive story lies broken in
pieces around us and cannot possibly be resuscitated. A few
quite cuddly survivors from before the Flood – antediluvians
indeed – still chunter on, mostly in the United States,
emitting smoke signals which speak of the growth of
liberty, the role of a freedom-guarding Parliament, the
wonders of democracy, but I can see no virtue in telling a
tale of demonstrable error for the sake of bringing English
history to our students, or indeed to anyone else. No: the
Stubbs–Pollard–Neale–Notestein–Morley–Arthur Bryant
tradition is dead and should remain decently buried: the
whigs have had their day.

It was not Butterfield who did for the whigs: the Indian
sign has been on them ever since Maitland, in his modestly

apologetic fashion, threw his bomb about the Parliament of 1305 into the ring, a bomb fitted with so slow a fuse that it took decades to explode properly. It may not now be recalled what resistance and contumely H. G. Richardson and George Sayles encountered when they took Maitland seriously and rewrote the history of the medieval Parliament by telling what have now become the commonplaces of our understanding. Perhaps they did not improve their chances of acceptance by the severity of their language, but the resistance was emotional and based on a liberal consensus. Oxford in particular would not surrender Stubbs, but Helen Cam, at some other place, also tried to save him. I am reminded of the misplaced zeal with which at this time so many historians, alleged revisionists among them, tell us that S. R. Gardiner never erred. In a way, there is special appropriateness in the accident that the demolition charge was laid by one who thought himself a lawyer. For this teleological history, which followed the rise of Parliament and freedom and which so powerfully attracted especially American historians, was really put together by lawyers who first organized it in the seventeenth century (replacing the sixteenth century's preoccupation with dynasties) and then imposed it with all the authority of the law. What a time it has taken us to shake off the shackles of the law – to make a reality of that emancipation of history from the lawyers which the separate creation of an historical tripos attempted to symbolize in 1875! However, we have our compensations. At long last Maitland's general guidance is being heeded and legal historians write historians', not lawyers', history. True, they tend to bewilder some lawyers, but (as they know very well) the guest bedrooms are being got ready in the mansion of history.

The abandoning of false trails should only lead to a search for more reliable roads. Here, however, the explorer does meet the real problems raised by the constant progress of research. What ever may today be true of British manufacturing industry, the productivity of the scholarly sector is awesome. The *Annual Bibliography* which I edit has now covered nine years, in which time we have added well over 25,000 items to the study of British and Irish history: and I cannot even claim absolutely total coverage. Not all those pieces, of course, are important, but some that do not themselves add to knowledge even more menacingly provide access to yet more new sources for it. New journals seem to appear every year: the last three years have witnessed the arrival of two concerned with representative institutions and three inviting discussions of the law and its social function. Old journals have grown at a rate of almost Israelian inflation. In 1958, when we dropped the prefix 'Cambridge' from the *Historical Journal*, the first volume ran to 207 pages; a quarter century later, volume 25 used up 1038. Not all this material pertains to English history, but a great deal does. There is assuredly an awful lot more of it to accommodate in the story, if ever it will actually be told, than faced the scholar just one generation ago.

A mere recital of bulk does not fully describe the problem. Much of that new history has been added outside the trusty old compartments of politics, administration, war and peace, though some of it – especially some endeavours in the history of the mind and of the fine arts – will cause no difficulties in the taking on of long stretches of English history. On the one hand, much social history will have to be incorporated: even plain economic history has been giving way to various forms of social studies. I will silence my doubts about much of that work on children, women and marriage; sometimes it does not seem overwhelmingly central to one's concerns. To cite two real and recent examples: will it matter to a history of England that someone has spent time on 'Single women in the London marriage market: age, status and mobility 1598–1619', and someone else on 'The regulation of sexuality since 1800'? Much social history has a charming quality of timelessness:

the facts of birth, copulation and death do not alter all that much through the ages – not nearly so much as some historians would like to believe. On the other hand, the study of crime or trade unions (the juxtaposition reveals my unconscious) does very definitely affect the way we look upon and understand the past, as do novel findings on peasant landholding in the thirteenth century or analyses of the distribution of wealth in the nineteenth. Much of this history, we should remember, will turn out to be provisional and even ephemeral. In the history of crime, for instance, at present a very popular genre, too much work tends to be weak on the law and strong on the author's social convictions: too often we meet there unhistorical purposes behind the work and somewhat dubious methods which suggest that we shall have to jettison ballast as well as acquire knowledge as we absorb the progress of research.

Revisionism is going on along the whole front of English history, and rightly so; but while some of it has already irremediably transformed many sectors, I rather think that a notable part of this new history will turn out to stand in need of revision itself, quite often back to square one. Not all exploded history will stay as dead as the parliamentary and puritan oppositions to Elizabeth I. An odd thing has happened to the poor of Elizabethan England, always known to be burdened with hard and horrid lives. However, we used to think that they were probably better off than their predecessors: there seemed to be signs to that effect. Of late, on the other hand, the period has been getting itself pigeonholed under the slogan 'pauperization of the poor' – a conviction that they were declining from a barely tolerable into a totally intolerable condition. These pauperized poor were bred out of mathematics, namely the discrepancy between the fast rise of prices and the slow rise of wages, rather than out of positive evidence. For some historians their existence survived the curious absence of the sort of consequences one would have expected to show up, such as famine, food riots, subsistence crises – all quite well vouched for in other countries. They survived the uncomfortable demonstration of quite positive improvements in the food supply. At this moment, however, they look like once again vanishing into the woodwork before a dawning suspicion that the apparently reliable calculation of wage rates does not accurately reflect the means of livelihood available to the lower orders of Elizabethan England. Shortly, I think, we shall not be forced to incorporate an element of major economic decline in a picture which also includes the great rebuilding of England and the signs of augmenting wealth well down the scale found in inventories and wills. Quite a few such seemingly awkward novelties may well disappear under further scrutiny: after all, historical knowledge rightly progresses as a rule in a dialectic of new notions and their limitations. The difficulty lies in knowing where to accept and where to doubt – and to do so without allowing the choice to be ruled by personal prejudice. But at any rate, while trying to keep up we also have to guard against a common and very understandable form of influenza: belief in the latest article.

However, when everything has been done to reduce the flood of innovation to a manageable size of reasonably reliable residues, one problem will remain to hamper the restoration of long stretches of English history to the place they ought to occupy in learning and in teaching. The present predilection for social and intellectual history operates against narrative, against the concept of a moving river of history. It studies the static elements in the stream – the boulders, the jammed tree-trunks, at best the eddies. Social analysis works by tactics which bring the stream to a halt, and it studies cross-sections. The French preceptors who prescribe these exercises have told us that they wish to make history stand still so that it can be analysed. I will not today contemplate any further this, to me, very odd endeavour which seems to suppose that history can be studied only by perverting its fundamental nature. But I draw your attention to the inadequacy of any historical analysis which is not predominantly directed towards an understanding of change through time. The present flood of historians' labours includes a great many contributions which not only, and quite rightly, study particular problems hard to incorporate in a story, but by the methods they favour positively inhibit our grasp of movement and transformation. I might add that by the language which so many of them employ they inhibit interest in history altogether. A history simply is not equal to a collection or even a sequence of technically analysed sociological states.

To sum up: any effort to seek a proper understanding of this country's past over some ten centuries faces present convictions which declare that such ambitions are intellectually mistaken and also irrelevant or even immoral in a world in which England no longer plays a major or exemplary role. Against this I set two counter-claims.

In the first place, the new history now produced must demand to be turned to historical purposes. The people who so diligently and often productively study it call it history; and they are right in this even when they fail to notice how their own methods stand in the way of truly historical thinking about the past. The undoubted fact that it has beome very difficult to write a history even of one century which is not hopelessly out of date on detail or superficial in its main concerns present no reason whatsoever for abandoning the task. Since unquestionably the people who lived through the experiences analysed by the historians of social structure, economic function, changing views on religion or magic, did live in England at identifiable points in time, it must be the task of the historian to incorporate the new knowledge in the older practice of continuous history. And in the second place I repeat what I said before. The long-term history of England continues to merit attention even though the empire is gone and we no longer wish to show off the Westminster Parliament as the last word in political wisdom. Without being in the least committed to a narrow and bigoted patriotism or blind to a wider world, one may still claim on good grounds, as I do, that special interest and importance attach to the history of a country whose past achievements were so formidable and influential – a country whose social, legal and political machineries differed so noticeably and so influentially from the practices of all other countries. It is right that the history of the rest of the world should be diligently studied and that some acquaintance with it should be brought to English students. But I am willing to maintain that we shall never properly understand the history of the last millennium unless we preserve and improve our understanding of the way in which over that long span of time the people and rulers of England – for most of that time a small and seemingly insignificant realm – managed their existence between those two inescapable reference points: the misery of birth and the certainty of death. And if we wish to understand this we shall have to study them in a continuum, not in portions or sections.

High claims, no doubt, and easy to assert, but can it not be done? If we can no longer fall back on a history of political progress, how shall we write the history of England? I can think of one or two themes, continuous or recurrent, around which it might be constructed, but I realize that to the demographer, the analyst and the specialist in the twentieth century they will probably appear superficial, even frivolous. (Not that frivolity should be deplored: one thing I have against the analysts is the deadly seriousness they apply to everything.) What other nation has gained and lost so many empires? Counting the Plantagenet effort, I make it three: perhaps there are more. What nation has more regularly recruited itself from other people and submerged their distinguishing characteristics – including the Welsh and Scottish neighbours? It is engaged in doing so once more today. It would be possible to write a good history of England

around her relations with the continent or around her peculiar law. These approximate suggestions all share the three
essential ingredients: they are interesting in themselves;
their proper understanding calls for a very extended time-
span; and they emphasize the difference that is England. So,
I admit, would a history of England written round the game
of cricket – and what monumentally tedious studies of social
structure that would bring in!

I should, however, quite seriously draw attention to one
element of continuity which is too rarely noticed. Until very
recently, the minds and attitudes of the English people were
ruled by two attempts to provide anchor-points of moderate
certainty in a manifestly uncertain and dangerous world.
The instruments were religion (reassurance in the hereafter)
and law (reassurance down here). Not everybody shared
identical views of either, and both changed a great deal in
the course of history: but they were always there, to frame
the way in which people regarded their existence. I feel a
certain duty incumbent upon me to call attention to these
fundamental embodiments of change and continuity because
I happen at present to be president of both the Ecclesiastical
History Society and the Selden Society – an engrossment of
offices which makes me feel much more sympathetic towards
Cardinal Wolsey. The experience has made me realize more
than ever I did before how central to the continuous history
of England are religion in one form or other and law in one
application or other – and how useful they both therefore
become in the writing of that continuous history on terms
which the depth of modern research demands. I really think
that they will serve much better than the ups and downs of
social mobility or the export trade: but they will be much
harder to manage properly.

If today we wish to grasp English history in the round, we
seek a history which remembers the existence of the people
who, in Thomas Smith's words, do not hold rule, and the
fact of the shires and boroughs away from the centre. It must

be the history of a whole society in active operation. I will confess to my preferred theme which will surprise no one but which is chosen because it would, I think, still make it possible to tie the detail on a continuous thread and embrace just about every aspect of this society without false artifice. That theme is government and politics – the manner in which this society managed to civilize power and order itself through constant changes. It is a history which cannot be properly written without regard for those continuous influences on the public and the private mind – religion and the law. It must attend to movement and change, escaping the falsely static impressions that would be left by a story built round strictly social and economic history which yet it cannot do without. A main thread spun out of the history of royal government and the law would necessarily incorporate the strands of particularity and localism; it would much more correctly present the growth of that peculiar English mixture of order and disorder, control and freedom, than would the traditional tale of Parliament; and it would be forced to remember all the people – governors as well as governed, clergy as well as laity, thieves as well as hangmen, husbandmen as well as philosophers, philistines as well as poets. Not to mention women as well as men. And since the prime interest of royal government has always looked to relations with other realms it would inevitably place England within the larger world, thus avoiding the dangers of insularity.

It is easy, or relatively easy, to list such notions; writing the story is another matter. After what I said about Acton's inaugural lecture, I ought to be more careful: I should not pretend to a skill I do not have. But remember that my starting point was the history we teach, not the history we write; and when we teach we do not expect to get everything in that should be in, nor do we expect one man to cover all the ground. But we do not teach well unless we compel attention to long stretches of English history. It is, I main-

tain, still as possible as it is necessary to allow the history of
England to form the backbone of that awareness of the past
which it is our duty to awake and maintain in others as well
as ourselves.

For let us not underestimate the task we face. I have today
been speaking in the main about the teaching of history,
especially at the universities, but I think we need to consider
much larger issues – issues larger than the possible end to
the employment of history graduates in schools. An age of
uncertainty, beset by false faiths and the prophets of constant innovation, badly needs to know its roots. Yet it is one
of the peculiarities of English society – one of the ways in
which it differs so much from other societies known to me –
that it largely lacks an active sense of history. The many
people who confuse conservatism and pageantry with a sense
of history will find this hard to believe, but it is a serious
truth about the English in the mass that they know very
little and care not greatly about their history. The past really
does not sit upon their backs, burdening the present; and if
you doubt this, I ask you to consider the Irish or the Scots,
the Germans or the Russians, not to mention the French
(certain that no other people has a history worth the name)
who have never ceased to behave as though Louis XIV or
Napoleon was still around. This quality of English life has
notable attractions. Because we in this country forget the
past almost as soon as it has become the past, we do not need
for ever to expiate it, avenge it, kiss its dead hand. But that
quality has equally notable drawbacks. When a past is
wanted for present uses, whether by way of reassurances or
for the justification of some new and drastic action, it is not
the real past that is wheeled into line but one constructed by
partisans for the use of the moment. The use of the moment
has its claims and can sometimes justly be responsible for
which part of the past gets emphasized. Ages dominated by
the Froude complex have needed the deflationary effects of a
history recording misdeeds and miseries. A *New Statesman*

era like ours, full of self-deprecation and envy, can do with the corrective of a part that demonstrates virtue and achievement. But we, as historians, do not write history for the use of the moment; we are the guardians and the distributors of the truths of history and should at least try to make sure than when current partisans plunder history for their own purposes they have a non-partisan and real history to stand over them. We neglect a duty if we do not treat the history of this country as a continuum worthy of discovery and a story worthy to be told.

The apprehensions which caused King George I to found this Regius chair are not absent from our lives. He, or his advisers, thought that a university curriculum dominated by the arid scholarship of classical learning failed to offer the nation that understanding of itself without which it could not hope to maintain and improve itself. Not all our current studies are as arid, or indeed as scholarly, as the humanities threatened to be in the age of Bentley. However, danger cones are flying. As the social scientists – a contradiction in terms – build their ahistorical models of a society that this or that operator would like to set up, to fulfil purposes which range from the fantasies of the unbalanced to the ignorant compassions of the uninstructed, the possibility grows rapidly that the problems we confront will be solved in ways totally destructive of what made England a country worth living in – a country worth coming to. I have said it before but it cannot be said often enough: it is one of the functions of the historian to prevent such disasters by telling the truth about the past without having it in mind to call up the past to come to the rescue of the present. Only if he avoids the temptations of devising comfortable theories and allegedly usable laws of human behaviour, only if he rejects all pontificating that puts the past tendentiously at the service of the present, will he in fact discharge his duty to that present. He serves best when he demonstrates the variety and unpredictability of the past and remembers all the world of humanity. There was a time when historians and teachers of history, conscious of insularity, rightly went forth to fetch home all the tea in China and all the quinine in Peru. Those harvests are gathered in and insularity is distant. Today, I hope, some of us will come back home and think home good enough to tell its long story to the world.

Index

128 *Index*